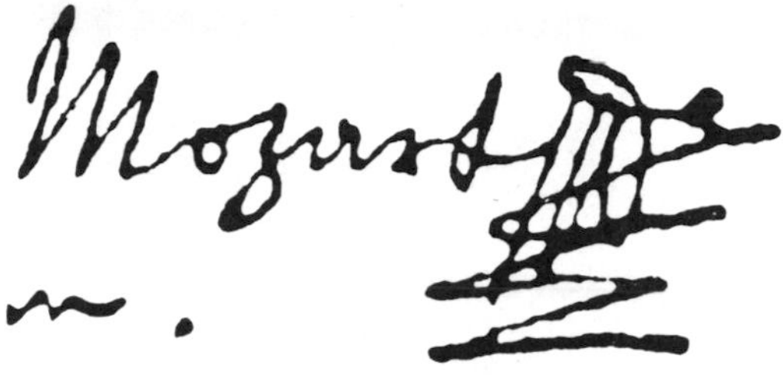
Mozart

MOZARTIANA

Two centuries of

Notes, Quotes, and Anecdotes

about

(Wolfgang) Amadeus Mozart

COLLECTED AND ILLUSTRATED BY
JOSEPH SOLMAN

Walker & Company
New York

First published in the United Kingdom in 1991 by Macmillan London Limited; first published in the United States of America in 1990 by Vintage Books, New York; first paperback edition published in 2002 by Walker Publishing Company, Inc.

Published simultaneously in Canada by Fitzhenry and Whiteside, Markham, Ontario L3R 4T8

For information about permission to reproduce selections from this book, write to Permissions, Walker & Company, 435 Hudson Street, New York, New York 10014

Library of Congress Cataloging-in-Publication Data

Mozartiana : two centuries of notes, quotes, and anecdotes about Wolfgang Amadeus Mozart / collected and illustrated by Joseph Solman.
    p. cm.
  ISBN 0-8027-7625-6 (pbk.)
    1. Mozart, Wolfgang Amadeus, 1756–1791—Anecdotes.
I. Solman, Joseph, 1909–

ML410.M9 M78   2002
780'.92—dc21   2002016773

Visit Walker & Company's Web site at www.walkerbooks.com

Printed in Canada

2 4 6 8 10 9 7 5 3

It may be that when the angels go about their task praising God, they play only Bach. I am sure, however, that when they are together *en famille* they play Mozart.

—KARL BARTH

CONTENTS

MOZARTIANA

INTRODUCTION

Sometime in the winter of 1930, a roommate who shared a studio apartment with my brother and me bought a recording of Mozart's Piano Concerto in G, K. 453. From the moment we put it on the battered, rickety Victrola, we all became entranced with its fluid beauty. It quickly replaced the well-worn Appassionata sonata of Beethoven as our daily religious service.

A great and growing passion for the instrumental music of Mozart ultimately led me to his operas. In the years following 1934, when John Christie began the Glyndebourne Festival in Sussex, recordings of Mozart's operatic works became popular with music lovers and radio stations—so much so that I found I could paint all afternoon listening to the sounds of *The Magic Flute* and *Figaro*, the music from the radio filling the room as the broad brush strokes of my street scenes filled the canvas.

As I became thus absorbed in his music, I decided to try a modern portrait of my idol. I checked the complete iconography of Mozart but soon discovered that the public craving for idealization of its great men had caused innumerable hacks to transform Mozart into a fair-haired Greek god. There were twenty-six portraits in all, most of them spurious, and no two seemed to give the same impression of what Wolfgang Mozart actually looked like. I did find a drawing from life done in 1789 by one Dora Stock that impressed me with its veracity and honesty. The jutting profile, the prominent nose, a soft, sensuous mouth with a hint of irony wrinkling it, a slightness of stature—all were there, a visual replica of the contemporary descriptions of Mozart that I'd read.

Using this portrait as my point of departure, I began making a number of sketches in pencil and watercolor. These, presented here in black-and-white, I offer as a kind of visual commentary on the many statements and stories about Mozart that I have collected over the years. In assembling them for this book I have discovered that reactions to Mozart are as abundant and unexpected as the rich variety found in the music itself. And the volume and fervor of these reactions are (at least to this surveyor) absolutely unparalleled in Western music and, with the possible exception of Shakespeare, in Western art.

For me, Mozart's music represents neither the prolonged sigh of faith that characterizes so much of the music written before his time, nor the stormy idealism which cloaks most music after him. Rather, he is that mercurial balance of the skeptic and the humane. Like him, and in him, we can always discover new worlds.

—JOSEPH SOLMAN
New York City

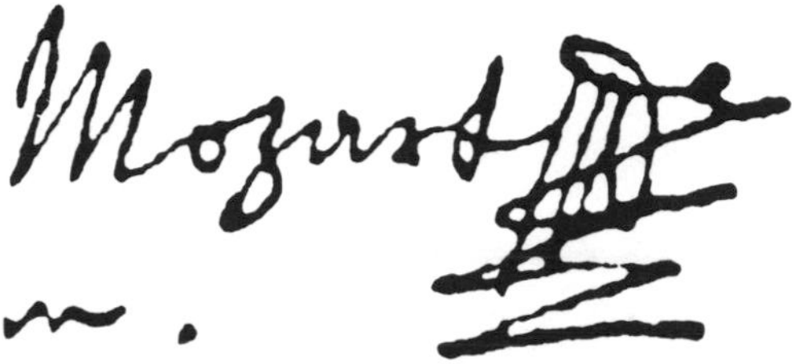
Mozart

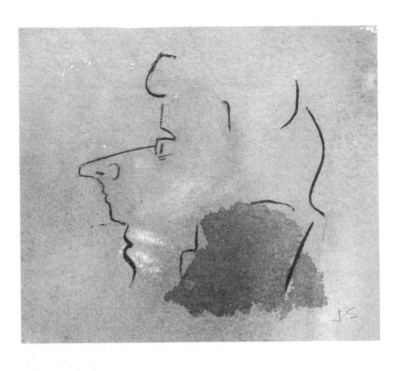

A Man, Just Like You

WOLFGANG AMADEUS

TAMINO: Tell me who you are, my jolly friend.

PAPAGENO: Who am I? Silly question! A man, just like you!

Sunday, January 27, 1756, 9 Getreidegasse, Salzburg, 8 P.M. A little boy is born to the violinist-composer Leopold Mozart and his wife, Anna Maria. One day later, the child is christened Johannes Chrysostomus Wolfgangus Theophilus Mozart. Chrysostomus ("Golden mouth") is rarely used; Theophilus becomes Gottlieb in German and Amadeus in Latin. Sigismundus is later added—perhaps to honor the archbishop of the city, the father's patron and employer.

1

He was a remarkably small man, very thin and pale, with a profusion of fine fair hair of which he was rather vain. He gave me a cordial invitation to his house, of which I availed myself, and passed a great part of my time there. He always received me with kindness and hospitality. He was remarkably fond of punch, of which beverage I have seen him take copious draughts. He was also fond of billiards and had an excellent billiard table in his house. Many and many a game have I played with him, but always came off second best. He gave Sunday concerts at which I was never missing. He was kind-hearted and always ready to oblige, but so very particular when he played that if the slightest noise were made, he instantly left off.　　—MICHAEL KELLY, the first Basilio in *The Marriage of Figaro*, in his *Reminiscences*

My brother was a rather pretty child.
—MARIA ANNA "NANNERL" MOZART, Wolfgang's sister, in a letter, 1799

Your countenance . . . was so grave that many intelligent persons, seeing your talent so early developed and your face always serious and thoughtful, were concerned for the length of your life.

—LEOPOLD MOZART, in a letter
to his son

I have made the acquaintance here of a certain Mr Mozard [*sic*], *maestro di capella* of the [Arch]bishop of Salzburg, a man of spirit, astute, experienced. . . . He has a daughter and a son. The former plays the harpsichord very well and the latter, who can't be more than twelve or thirteen, even at that age composes and is a *maestro di musica.* I've seen compositions which appear to be his and certainly they are not bad and not such as I would expect to find in a boy of twelve. . . . Moreover the boy is good-looking, vivacious, gracious and very well mannered; when you make his ac-

A Man, Just Like You 3

quaintance, it is difficult not to like him. Certainly he will become a prodigy if as he grows older he continues to make the necessary progress.

—JOHANN ADOLPH HASSE,
composer, in a letter,
September 30, 1769

When Mozart was seven, four of his violin and piano sonatas were published. The dedication, to the second daughter of Louis XV, Princess Victoire, reads: *"Votre très humble, très obéissant, et très petit serviteur, W.M."*

Because of Mozart, it's all over after age seven.
—WENDY WASSERSTEIN

We are told that Mozart, dragged all over Europe from the age of six, exhibited like a performing dog before kings, overloaded with flattery, presents and kindness, often asked those who seemed interested in him the naïve question, "Do you love me?" It was his greatest need. Even before his genius had time to mature, he was discarded like a plaything which no longer amused. At each stage of his life he had to be remade. With each proof, a new proof was required.

"Do you love me? Do you really love me?" Yes, Wolfgang Amadeus, as much as I can. More than any master in any art. More than all human genius. More than all human perfection.

—HENRI GHEON, *In Search of Mozart*

One of these visits found the six-year-old Mozart at the Viennese royal palace. He was presented to the Empress Maria Theresa and promptly jumped into her lap and asked for a kiss. He played with her daughter, seven-year-old Marie Antoinette. One morning, he slipped on the polished floor and the little princess helped him to his feet. Mozart told her, *"When I grow up, I'm going to marry you!"*

In 1777, when Mozart was twenty-one, he met Aloysia Weber, a beautiful girl

A Man, Just Like You 5

of sixteen with an extraordinary voice. At their first meeting, she sang the de Amicis arias from his *Lucio Silla*. Mozart fell deeply in love and composed for her many of his concert arias—often very difficult showpieces.

I like an aria to fit a singer as perfectly as a well-tailored suit of clothes.

> —MOZART, in a letter to his father, February 28, 1778

On Christmas Day, 1778, Mozart was rushing back to Aloysia after a long concert tour. But when he arrived late that afternoon at the Webers' flat, he found her surrounded by a group of admirers. Aloysia ignored him; he turned away. Many feel that Mozart never had a moment of romantic passion after that day, though certainly he loved his wife, Aloysia's younger sister Constanze.

As an old woman, Aloysia was

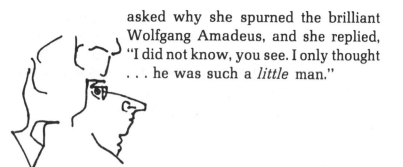

asked why she spurned the brilliant Wolfgang Amadeus, and she replied, "I did not know, you see. I only thought . . . he was such a *little* man."

In 1813, when I was in Dresden, I once met Luigi Bassi, that old *buffo,* for whom, twenty-six years earlier, Mozart had written the roles of Don Giovanni, and of Almaviva in *Figaro.*

"Mr. Mozart was an extremely eccentric and absent-minded young man, but not without a certain spirit of pride. He was very popular with the ladies, in spite of his small size; he had a most unusual face, and he could cast a spell on any woman with his eyes. . . ." On this subject, Bassi told me three or four little anecdotes. Which, however, I must refrain from including at this point.

—Stendhal, *Life of Rossini*

Mozart as a youth was rather thin; but he afterwards inclined rather to stoutness. He was somewhat below

A Man, Just Like You 7

medium height; what his exact stature was in feet and inches, we have not been able to ascertain: about 5 feet 5½ inches we are inclined to estimate it. . . . His head, a trifle large in proportion to his height, was of goodly shape; and he had a profuse allowance of fine hair—of lightish brown shade in his early years, but which grew darker by degrees. His nose was formed upon a rather too liberal scale, and . . . his eyes were of a clear, decided blue. . . .

In respect to Mozart's ears, it appears that there was an abnormality of shape in one of these members—the left ear namely; that convolution of the outer which is known as the *Concha* was deficient altogether; and it would further appear that this peculiar defect was inherited by Mozart's younger son.

—E. J. Breakespeare, Life of Mozart

It is a peculiar irony of fate that the man whose inner ear has, so to speak, the highest human development has a retarded and malformed outer ear.

—P. H. Gerber, 1898

"Mozart ear" has a round and sometimes almost square appearance ... the upper half of the ear is flat [and] the ear lobe is ill developed or absent ... the general prevalence in a hospital population seems to be less than one in a 1000. ... Who first gave this striking but rare abnormality its present eponym? Gerber's paper [was] published in a widely read clinical journal [but] justification for the label seems to be scant.

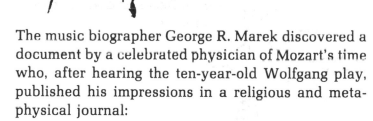

—PAXTON, PAHOR, and GRAHAM, M.D.s., "Medicine and Music," *British Medical Journal*

The music biographer George R. Marek discovered a document by a celebrated physician of Mozart's time who, after hearing the ten-year-old Wolfgang play, published his impressions in a religious and metaphysical journal:

Gentlemen, without doubt you have heard the young Mozart. ... You have seen with astonishment a nine-year-old child who plays the piano like the great masters. You have heard with greater astonishment the testimony of trustworthy persons that he played excellently when he was three years old. You will recognize that everything he plays is composed by himself and that all pieces played by him, including his free fantasies, show that power which is the telltale mark of genius. . . .

The musician receives at his birth such a precise and fine ear that the least false tone gives him pain, just as the ear of the true poet is offended immediately by a bad verse. . . . The sensitivity and precision of young Mozart's ear are so great that false tones or those which are too sharp or too heavy cause tears to spring to his eyes. This still very young child is quite natural and utterly charming. He has extraordinary knowledge of music, but if he were not a musician, he would probably be a very ordinary child. . . . His heart is as sensitive as his ear.

—Dr. S.A.A. Tissot,
Aristide, 1766

The court trumpeter of Salzburg at the time of Mozart's youth, Andreas Schachtner, was a great friend of the Mozart family. In his letters, he told many stories of the young Mozart that have since become legendary. On one occasion, when little Wolferl was playing on a small violin, he announced that Schachtner's instrument "was just half a quarter of a tone sharper than mine." Mozart was able to tell the difference in pitch between the two instruments to an eighth of a tone.

But Wolferl had never had a lesson on that violin. Schachtner relates how the four-year-old child came into the room one morning when Leopold and three of his friends were practicing a string quartet. Mozart was holding his new violin under his arm and begged to play with them—the second violin part. Wolferl stands in the corner and plays along with the group, but soon the second violinist puts down his instrument. The little boy is playing the part better than he is....

I said to the boy, that I should be glad to hear an extemporary *Love Song*, such as his friend Manzoli might choose in an opera. The boy on this looked back with much archness, and immediately began five or six lines of a jargon recitative proper to introduce a love song.

He then played a symphony which might correspond with an air composed to the single word *Affeto*.

It had a first and second part, which, together with the symphonies, was of the length that opera songs generally last: if this extemporary composition was not amazingly capital, yet it showed the most extraordinary readiness of invention.

Finding that he was in humour, and as it were inspired, I then desired him to compose a *Song of Rage*, such as might be proper for the opera stage.

The boy again looked back with much archness, and began five or six lines of a jargon recitative proper to precede a *Song of Anger*. This lasted also about the same time as *Song of Love;* and in the middle of it, he had worked himself up to such a pitch, that he beat his harpsichord like a person possessed, rising sometimes in his chair. The word he pitched upon for this second extemporary composition was *Perfido.*

—Hon. Daines Barrington (1727–1800), lawyer, antiquary, lettrist, in a paper on musical prodigies; from *The Mozart Companion,* by Gerald Abraham

Mozart wrote everything with such ease and speed as might at first be taken for carelessness or haste; also he never went to the pianoforte while composing. His imagination held before him the whole work clear and lively once it was conceived. His great knowledge of composition made easy for him the general harmonic panorama. One seldom finds in his scores improved or erased passages. But it does not follow that he merely sketched out his works hastily. The composition had long been finished in his head before he sat himself at his writing-desk. . . . Consequently the writing was for him an easy task during which he often joked and chattered.

—Franz Niemetschek,
first biographer of Mozart,
Life of Mozart, 1798

People err who think my art comes easily to me. I assure you, dear friend, nobody has devoted so much time and thought to composition as I. There is not a famous master whose music I have not industriously studied through many times.

—Mozart

He wrote music like letters and never tried a movement until it was finished. . . . He was always strumming on something—his hat, his watch fob, the table, the chair, as if they were the keyboard.

—Constanze Mozart

14   Mozartiana

In 1779, Wolfgang and his father were in Rome during Holy Week. Leopold took him to the Sistine Chapel to hear the famous *Miserere* by Gregorio Allegri, a complex choral work for nine voices. This sacred piece of music was so worshipped that it was forbidden, under pain of excommunication, to copy it, or to remove any part thereof. Mozart heard the work once, then rushed back to his rooms, where he wrote out the entire piece from memory. This amazing feat created a great sensation in Rome. When a few days later he heard a second performance of the *Miserere,* he checked it against his manuscript—to find there were very few, very minor mistakes.

Mozart relates to his father in a letter of April 8, 1781: *"Today (for I am writing at eleven o'clock at night) we had a concert, where three of my compositions were performed—new ones, of course: a rondo for a concerto for Brunetti; a sonata with violin accom-*

paniment for myself, which I composed last night between eleven and twelve (but in order to be able to finish it, I only wrote out the accompaniment for Brunetti and retained my own part in my head); and then a rondo for Ceccarelli, which he had to repeat."
The autograph of this sonata for piano and violin (K. 379) bears out Mozart's statement: the violin part is written in a light yellowish shade of ink; the piano part, however, is notated in shorthand with the same shade of ink and later traced in dark ink, when Mozart had time to complete the piano score.

—ERICH HERTZMANN, from an address delivered for the Mozart bicentennial at Columbia University, New York City

Never was Mozart less recognizably a great man in his conversation and actions than when he was busied with an important work. . . . Either he intentionally concealed his inner tension behind superficial frivolity, for reasons which could not be fathomed, or he took delight in throwing into sharp contrast the divine ideas of his music and these sudden outbursts or vulgar attitudes, and in giving himself pleasure by seeming to make fun of himself. I can understand that so exalted an artist can, out of a deep veneration for his Art, belittle and as it were expose to ridicule his own personality.　　　—JOSEPH LANGE, brother-in-law of Mozart, in his *Reminiscences*, Vienna, 1808

They could always say that they had not heard him . . . that it was all prearranged; that it was ridiculous to think that he could compose, and so forth. . . . But I caught one of those people nicely. Our friend was to hand this person a most extraordinarily difficult concerto, which was to be put before little Wolfgang twelve years old. So the fellow had the opportunity, therefore, of hearing his concerto played by Wolfgang as if he knew it by heart. The amazement of this composer and clavier-player was immense. . . . He finally declared: "All I can say as an honest person is that this boy is the greatest man now living in the world. It was impossible to believe it!"

—Leopold Mozart, in a letter to Johann Lorenz Hagenauer, February 1768

Once, in Geneva, I met a child who could play everything at sight. His father said to me before the assembled company: So that no doubt shall remain as to my son's talent, write for him, for tomorrow, a very difficult Sonata movement. I wrote him an allegro in E flat; difficult but unpretentious; he played it, and everyone, except myself, believed it was a miracle. The boy did not stop; but following the modulations, he substituted a quantity of passages for those which I had written.

—André Ernest Modeste Grétry, *Mémoires ou Essaies sur la Musique*, 1795

Then I came out, all by myself and played the last sonata, in D, for Dürnitz [K. 284], then my Concerto in B-flat, then again by myself a fugue in C minor, in the organ style, and then all at once I invented a magnificent sonata in C right out of my head, with a rondeau to end it. It made a great effect and racket. Herr Stein, the piano maker, could only make faces and grimaces in admiration.

—MOZART, in a letter to his
father, October 22, 1777

The riddle of Mozart is precisely that "the man" refuses to be a key for solving it. In death, as in life, he conceals himself behind his work.

—WOLFGANG HILDESHEIMER,
Mozart

On February 9, 1784, Mozart began to enter in a little notebook of forty-four pages all his works as he completed them, dating them and indicating the beginning of each work on two staves. He continued this practice till shortly before his death. . . .

In three years, from 1784 through 1786, he composed no less than fifty-six works, including twelve of his greatest piano concertos, two piano quartets, four of his major string quartets, his fantasia and piano sonata in C minor, and numerous other vocal and instrumental works, culminating in *The Marriage of Figaro* and the "Prague" symphony.

—ALFRED EINSTEIN, *Mozart:*
His Character, His Work

Wolfgang Mozart's "Häuschen," Rauhensteingasse 8, the summer cottage outside of Vienna where he composed *The Magic Flute,* was moved to Salzburg in 1877. Inscribed on the monument outside, beneath a bust of Mozart cut in granite:

Jung gross	(Grand youth,
Spät erkannt	Long unrecognized,
Nie erreicht	Never acknowledged)

Really a Good Fellow

MOZART'S CONTEMPORARIES

BELMONTE: He really is a good fellow.

OSMIN: His head should be on a spike!

This boy will consign us all to oblivion!
>   —JOHANN ADOLPH HASSE,
>   composer and contemporary
>   of Mozart, after hearing his
>   opera *Ascanio in Alba*
>   performed in Milan, 1771

This music, so harmonious and so lofty in inspiration,
so pure, both soft and sorrowful . . . made me forget
as I listened to it my past woes and those that the
future held perhaps in store for me.
>   —ABBÉ MARTINANT DE PRENEUF,
>   1797

I think I told you that the young Mozart is here; that he is less of a miracle though always the same miracle. But then he will never be anything but a miracle, and that is all. —ABBÉ GALIANI, in a letter to Madame d'Epinay, 1769, when Mozart was thirteen

From these two [the quartets K. 421 and K. 465] we can decide that the composer, whom I do not know and do not want to know, is only a clavier player with a depraved ear: he follows that false system that divides the octave into twelve semitones.

—GIUSEPPE SARTI (1729–1802)

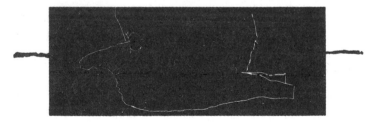

In January 1787, the Viennese correspondent of the *Magazin der Musik* reported of Mozart: "He is the best piano player I have ever heard; but it is a pity that in his ingenious and really beautiful compositions he goes too far in his attempt to be new, so that feeling and sentiment are little cared for. His new quartets, dedicated to Haydn, are too strongly spiced—and what palate can stand that for long?"

—MAX GRAF, *composer and critic*

These six quartets dedicated to Haydn, finished in 1785, were sent back from the printer to the publisher, Artaria, because they contained so many "misprints." But the music had been correctly transcribed; these "errors" were unfamiliar dissonances and chords. When the Hungarian prince Grassalkowitsch had the work performed, he thought the musicians were playing miserably and he stormed up to them in disgust. When he saw they were playing the music as written, he tore the sheet music to bits.

This great master [Mozart], because of his early acquaintance with harmony, has come to know it so deeply and inwardly that the unpracticed ear has difficulty in following him in his works. Even practiced ones must hear his pieces several times.

—ERNST LUDWIG GERBER, chamber musician to the Prince of Schwarzburg, from his *Old Lexicon*, 1790— a year before Mozart's death

He produced works that seemed to differ widely from everything that had heretofore been heard and seen ... filled with a richness of invention and beauty that only a few could elucidate—the majority could only feel. . . . What he vouchsafed us in his brief sojourn on earth was great and lofty enough to border often upon the inconceivable. . . . He was a meteor on the musical horizon, for whose appearance we were not yet prepared. —ERNST LUDWIG GERBER,

less than fifteen years later

How can this music, so full of force, majesty, and grandeur, be expected to please the lovers of ordinary opera? The grand and noble qualities of the music in *Don Giovanni* will appeal only to the small minority of the elect. It is not such as to tickle the ear of the crowd. —SCHINK, a contemporary of

Mozart, writing in the
Dramaturische Monate, 1790

The golden mean, the truth, is no longer recognized or valued. To win applause one must write stuff so simple that a coachman might sing it, or so incomprehensible that it pleases simply because no sensible man can comprehend it.

—MOZART, in a letter to his father, 1782

He is too *sincere,* not active enough, too susceptible to illusions, too little aware of the means of achieving success. Here, [Paris] in order to succeed, one must be artful, enterprising and bold; for the sake of his fortunes, I could wish [Wolfgang] had half as much talent and twice as much of the qualities I have described. . . . You may see, my dear Sir, that in a country where all the mediocre and detestable musicians have made immense fortunes, your son could not manage at all.

—BARON FRIEDRICH MELCHIOR GRIMM, in a letter to Leopold Mozart, 1778

It was in that year that Mozart's mother died, in a small attic apartment off the Faubourg Saint-Honoré, a cold, dark flat too small to fit even a clavier. Mozart retained throughout his life a hatred of France and things French.

What amount of fee Mozart received for his performances in private we have no means of ascertaining; in general, however, the aristocracy were accustomed to reward distinguished artists according to their deserts, and the exceptional position of the Viennese nobility enabled the artists to accept their liberality without loss of dignity; the more so as it was founded on true esteem. The friendly demeanor of persons of high rank was highly prized by the artists; nor would there be wanting some who sought to merit it by servile adulation. From any tint of this Mozart was absolutely free; not only was he unfettered by the forms of social class distinctions, but he moved in society with all the independence of a distinguished man, without laying claim to the license

Really a Good Fellow 29

often accorded to artists of genius. The etiquette of rank was no bar to his intimacy with Prince Karl Lichnowsky; and another of his true friends was Count August Hatzfeld, who was a first-rate violinist, playing with Mozart in the latter's quartets.

—OTTO JAHN, *W. A. Mozart*

Salzburg is perhaps the international capital of "Mozartiana." But Mozart, remembering his unhappy days in that city, might laugh ironically at the countless souvenirs bearing his name. His notorious runins with his Salzburg employer, the Archbishop Colloredo, are furiously described in his letters:

Still, I must frankly confess that I should arrive in Salzburg with a lighter heart if I were not aware that I am to be in the service of the court. It is that thought which is intolerable to me. Consider it yourself—put yourself in my place! At Salzburg I never know how I stand. I am to be everything—and yet nothing. Nor do I ask so much nor so little—I just want something—I mean to be something!

—MOZART, in a letter to his father, October 15, 1778

The Archbishop cannot recompense me for the slavery in Salzburg! . . . [He] must not attempt to put on grand airs with me as he used to; it is not impossible, it is even likely that I would put my fingers to my nose—and I know full well that you would enjoy this as much as I would! —MOZART, in a letter to his father, November 12, 1778

Finally, at the beginning of May [1781], when Mozart presented an . . . excuse for not returning from Vienna

Really a Good Fellow 31

to Salzburg on a certain day ... there was an explosion. Colloredo scolded his court organist roughly, and told him in anger that he could go to the devil. Mozart took that as a formal invitation to ask for his dismissal; but his request was not accepted by Count Karl Arco.... On the occasion of one attempt to get his memorandum accepted—it was the third he had written—Mozart was literally kicked out the door by Count Arco. —ALFRED EINSTEIN, *Mozart: His Character, His Work*

Salzburg is nothing now to me except an opportunity to give the Count a kick, even if it were in the public street. —MOZART, in a letter to his father, Vienna, June 1781

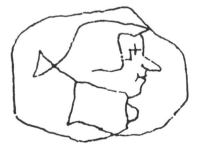

The great and fiery spirit that pervades his work and the overwhelming feeling he shows overpower with irresistible force.... Whoever has once found Mozart to his taste will find little satisfaction in other music.

—Franz Niemetschek,
Life of Mozart, 1798

Mozart is undoubtedly one of the greatest of original geniuses, and I have never known any other composer to possess such an amazing wealth of ideas. I wish he were not so spendthrift with them. He does not give the listener time to catch his breath, for no sooner is one inclined to reflect upon a beautiful inspiration than another appears, even more splendid, which drives away the first, and this continues on and on, so that in the end one is unable to retain any of these beauties in the memory

—Karl Ditters von
Dittersdorf, composer,
contemporary of Mozart, in
his *Autobiography*

If any fault had to be found in Mozart, it could surely be only this: that such abundance of beauty almost tires the soul, and the effect of the whole is sometimes obscured thereby. But happy the artist whose only fault lies in all too great perfection.

—UNNAMED REVIEWER OF
Don Giovanni, Berlin, 1791

A Leipzig publisher once wrote to Mozart: "Write in a more popular style, or I can neither print nor pay for anything of yours!" Mozart's reply: *"Fine! I'll earn nothing more, go hungry—and the devil if I care!"*

You wish me to write an *opera buffa* for you. Most willingly, if you are inclined to have a vocal composition of mine for yourself alone, but if with a view to produce it on the stage at Prague, I cannot in that case comply with your wish, all my operas being too closely connected with our personal circle, so they could never produce the proper effect. . . . But even then I should risk a great deal, for scarcely any man could stand beside the great Mozart.

I only wish I could impress on every friend of

mine, and on great men in particular, the same depth of musical sympathy and profound appreciation of Mozart's inimitable music that I myself feel and enjoy; then nations would vie with each other to possess such a jewel within their frontiers. . . . It enrages me to think that the unparalleled Mozart is not yet engaged by some imperial or royal court! Forgive my excitement, but I love the man so dearly!

—FRANZ JOSEPH HAYDN, in a letter to Herr Roth, 1787

It was not long before various composers came to me for libretti. But there were only two in Vienna whom I considered worthy of my respect, Martin, the composer at that time favoured by the Emperor Joseph, and W. Mozart. Although endowed with talents superior perhaps to those of any other composer in the world, past, present or future, Mozart, whose acquaintance I had made at the house of Baron Wetzlar, his great admirer and friend, had never been able to display his heaven-sent genius at Vienna, thanks to the plots of his enemies. . . . I can never recall without rejoicing that it was in great part to my own perseverance alone that Europe and the whole world owe the delightful vocal music of this wonderful genius.

—LORENZO DA PONTE, Mozart's librettist for *The Marriage of Figaro, Don Giovanni,* and *Così Fan Tutte*

A painter, hoping to flatter Domenico Cimarosa [1749–1801], told him that he was the greatest of composers, superior even to Mozart. . . . "What would you think, sir," said Cimarosa, "of a musician who told you you were superior to Raphael?"

—ETHAN MORDDEN,
Opera Anecdotes

Mozart, you are a god.

—ANTONIO SALIERI, in the play *Mozart and Salieri,* by Aleksandr Pushkin

God needed Mozart to let himself into the world.
—ANTONIO SALIERI, in the play
Amadeus, by Peter Shaffer

I believe Salieri must have responded to Mozart the way most artists do—with amazement, humility, envy and finally with gratitude. For, in the end, the source of creation is available to all of us, and those who are blessed with genius are only messengers bringing good news to an otherwise dark, at times unbearable, world.   —F. MURRAY ABRAHAM

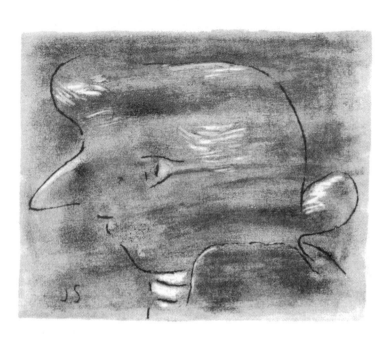

Changing Their Minds

THE CHANGING VIEW OF MOZART

DON ALFONSO: What grimaces, what affectations!
. . . People of that kind are always the first to
change their minds.

Mozart's influence transcends history. Each generation sees something different in his work. . . . Mozart's
music, which to so many of his contemporaries still
seemed to have the brittleness of clay, has long since
been transformed into gold gleaming in the light,
though it has taken on the different luster of each new
generation. . . . No earthly remains of Mozart survived
save a few wretched portraits, no two of which are
alike; the fact that all the reproductions of his death-
mask, which would have shown him as he really was,
have crumbled to bits seems symbolic. It is as though
the world-spirit wished to show that here is pure
sound, conforming to a weightless cosmos, trium-

phant over all chaotic earthliness, spirit of the world-spirit.   —ALFRED EINSTEIN, *Mozart:*
                              His Character, His Work

On the whole, Mozart is still *terra incognita:* for who knows and who plays his 650 works? Whereas one doesn't miss one semiquaver of a certain Dr. Johannes, whether it is for *clarinetto* or *contra fagotto!*
                              —FERRUCCIO BUSONI,
                              October 7, 1917

Mozart, a delicate and lovable soul, but quite eighteenth century, even when he is serious.
                              —FRIEDRICH NIETZSCHE,
                              The Will to Power

Around the beginning of our century, we find the "rediscovery" of Mozart, which has only been intensified through the propagation of chaotic music and the obvious necessity which follows to return to real beauty and greatness in music. . . . I can remember

when one of his symphonies was used to fill up an empty space in a programme where the main dishes were Beethoven, Wagner, etc. He was thought of as a trinket, charming, delicious, yes—but a trinket all the same. —PABLO CASALS,
Conversations with Casals

When I was a young conductor, musicians all loved Mozart and wanted to play him, but the directors of the Opera were very much against it. It was not box office. For instance, in Riga, I remember very well that one of the Board, when he found out that the box office was not so very great, said we must give better pieces! And then through Mahler's efforts in Vienna, Mozart was seen in a new aspect. His dramatic veracity was acknowledged and Mozart *became* box office . . . and later on, I continued this line in Munich. I was ten years in Munich and of course I served the cause of Mozart very much. . . . He became one of the great drawing cards of the Opera in Munich. And then later I once more came to Vienna and took up the directorship of the Vienna Opera from 1935 until Hitler came. But by this time, Mozart had become real box office. More than Verdi, more than Wagner.
—BRUNO WALTER

As the [nineteenth] century proceeded, Mozart was interpreted more and more in the spirit of Beethoven and Wagner; all music had to be treated as philosophy and religion, until the even more devastating period of psychoanalysis arrived to insist upon the "problematic" and "daemonic" aspects of sex. It has been for our own century and for the generation of the present day to rediscover Mozart, not as the expression of an imaginary age of innocence, still less as the musical illustrator of an equally imaginary century of rococo artificiality, but as the completely mature creator of music that we can still enjoy as a thing of delight for its own sake.

—Edward J. Dent, *Mozart's Operas: A Critical Study*

I then took in hand a short Mozart Cycle which included *Il Seraglio, Le Nozze di Figaro, Così Fan Tutte,* and *Il Impresario.* Of the four works *Così Fan*

Tutte proved easily the most interesting; few had ever heard of it, and fewer still seemed acquainted with the music, although it is equal in beauty to anything the composer ever wrote. As one lovely melody followed another until it seemed as if the invention of Mozart was inexhaustible . . . it was hard to believe that in our age of vaunted culture and education a work like this, then one hundred and twenty years old, was being heard almost for the first time in a great city like London.

—THOMAS BEECHAM

I had, in 1939, decided to dedicate my life to Haydn, of whose music there was, in those days, no collected edition; indeed, only one-tenth had ever been published at all. Yet I always considered Mozart something quite alone and beyond other music, including Bach, Beethoven and Wagner. I ought to say that this view was then considered not merely eccentric but almost lunatic.   —H. C. ROBBINS LANDON,
Mozart's Last Year

Changing Their Minds 43

The Iturbi debut was made with the Mozart Concerto in D Minor (K. 466) and the fact of its selection was interesting. Iturbi was one of three pianists . . . to play a Mozart concerto that season [1930] in New York, and Olin Downes thought this constituted "an extraordinary symptom of the return of classicism." The Mozartian vogue was curious, at least on the surface, for it had little obvious connection with the prevailing symphonic modes of the time. Downes thought it was for that very reason that the audience exulted in the "very pure Mozart melody, very clean Mozartian form and orchestration." Another segment of the listeners, undoubtedly influenced by the neo-classicists, certainly enjoyed Mozart for precisely the same reasons that they enjoyed the predominant modern compositional idiom. They perceived the connection between Mozart and certain contemporary writers of "pure" music. In one way the two groups came together—both were in reaction against the romanticism that had dominated the concert hall in the days before World War I. And one of the great things about the Twenties and early Thirties was the rediscovery of Bach and Mozart after their long internment beneath the mountains of nineteenth-century sound. Even if the composers who have shaped the modern musical sensibility turn out, in the

end, to be only minor figures, we will owe to their aesthetic the rediscovery and the revaluation of Mozart and his predecessors. —RICHARD SCHICKEL,
The World of
Carnegie Hall

It has become the custom to treat this most sublime of all tonal masters as a "rococo artist," to represent his work as the epitome of the ornamental and the playful. Though it is correct to say that he was one who solved all "problems" before they were even posed, that in him passion is divested of everything earthly and seems to be viewed from a bird's eye perspective, it is equally true that his work contains—even when transfigured, spiritualized and liberated from reality—all phases of human experience, from the monumental, dark grandeur of the Commandant's scene in *Don Giovanni* to the daintiness of the Zerlina arias, the heavenly frivolities of *Figaro,* and the deliberate ironies of *Così Fan Tutte.*
—RICHARD STRAUSS

Changing Their Minds 45

As with all great creators, the secret of his beauty is not fully revealed at first sight; however, we cannot help being astonished that it has needed nearly a century and a half for people to discover in Mozart anything other than grace and charming elegance. This miraculous artist, as Teodor de Wyzewa used to style him, in his last symphonies does in fact reveal to us the true world inhabited by his soul at the moment when it is turning toward other regions.

—GEORGES DE SAINT-FOIX,
The Symphonies of Mozart

Of all musicians Mozart is the one from whom our epoch has taken us farthest away; he speaks only in a whisper, and the public has ceased to hear anything but shouts.   —ANDRÉ GIDE, *Journals*

One indisputable fact, we believe, results from our study: in Mozart's artistic existence there was not only development of technique; there was also growth in thought. We are far from thinking that no one before us had noticed the organic quality of his work, considered in time; no one who has soaked himself in the composer's music has failed to recognize it. But the opinion that Mozart never grew up and merely repeated himself, with an unconsciousness that some profess to find charming, all through his life, is so slow in dying that we are glad to carry yet another slab to its grave.

—C. M. GIRDLESTONE,
Mozart's Piano Concertos

The past is never, as our jargon implies, a fixed quantity; it is in movement. . . . Mozart, for his contemporaries, was not the serene classic, the apostle of measure and perfection that so many of his nineteenth century admirers, and even some today, have liked to conjure up. On the contrary, he was for them a painter of intense and even sombre canvases, of large scope and vast design.

—ROGER SESSIONS, *Lectures*

Changing Their Minds 47

Within living memory Mozart has turned from a gay, superficial composer to a profound and tragic one.

—JACQUES BARZUN,
The Score magazine

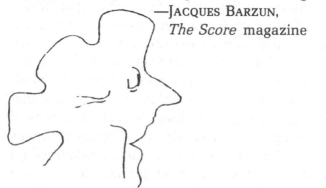

We have in the course of the last half-century changed our receptivity toward Mozart and Bach. Mozart, who in sheer beauty brought music to its purest sheen, has become more mysterious. Bach, that magnificently intricate genius, has become more "human."   —GEORGE MAREK, *Beethoven*

Fifty years this [the idea that Mozart was merely a rococo composer] was what most people thought about him, and the notion was supported by horrible little plaster casts which made him look the perfect eighteenth-century dummy. I bought one of those busts when I was at school, but when I heard the G minor Quintet, I realized that it could not have been written by the smooth, white character on my mantelpiece and threw the bust in the wastepaper basket. . . . His formal perfection was used to express two characteristics which were very far from the rococo style. One of them was that peculiar kind of melancholy, a melancholy amounting almost to panic, which so often haunts the isolation of genius. Mozart felt it quite young. The other characteristic was almost the opposite: a passionate interest in human beings, and in the drama of human relationships. How often in his orchestral pieces—concertos or quartets—we find ourselves participating in a drama or dialogue; and of course this feeling reaches its natural conclusion in opera.

—KENNETH CLARK, *Civilisation*

When Mozart wrote *Don Giovanni*, it was not cute and it was not charming. If you put yourself back with the first audience that heard that piece in the 1780s— music of comparable violence as the opening notes of *Don Giovanni* had never been heard in the history of the world. That was shattering music for the audience. And we now think of Mozart as "a rest for the soul" and "something lovely." In fact, for his first audience it was tough, it was shocking, people said this is too intellectual, people said this is too forceful, it's too brutal, can't it be a little *nicer?*

But it wasn't intended to go down easy. Mozart himself was deeply committed to a wide range of social issues. . . . In *Don Giovanni* you don't have all of the cast members come to the front of the stage . . . and sing, at the top of their lungs, in a C major military march *"Viva la libertà!"* two years before the French Revolution—thirteen times, which is how often they sing it—if you don't actually intend to push your public. —PETER SELLARS, as quoted on Bill Moyers' "A World of Ideas"

It is a long time since a pilgrimage to Central Europe was necessary in order to hear Mozart in abundance. Who could have predicted that almost all of Mozart's six hundred and twenty-six works would now exist on records? That every summer in New York there is a whole month of daily Mostly Mozart concerts, which draw audiences so appreciative, motley, and contemporary as to make Mozart a sign of these times as well as of all time? Mozart lives with us in all our variegations of humanity. I think we love him, among our other reasons, for his versatility, unmatched by any other composer in all music.

—MARCIA DAVENPORT, "A Note for 1979," preface to *Mozart*

From Your Wisdom

COMPOSERS ON MOZART

FIGARO: We are the first to benefit from your wisdom.

I tell you before God and as an honest man that your son is the greatest composer known to me; he has taste and in addition the most complete knowledge of composition.   —FRANZ JOSEPH HAYDN,

to Mozart's father, Leopold, after hearing the six quartets Mozart dedicated to him in 1785

Mozart sent these six quartets to Haydn with the following letter:

To my dear friend Haydn:

A father who had decided to send his sons into the great world, thought it his duty to entrust them to the protection and guidance of a man who was very celebrated at the time and who, in addition, happened to be his best friend.

Here, then, I am sending my six sons to you, most celebrated and very dear friend. They are indeed the fruit of long and laborious study; but many friends have given me the hope that these children may one day be a source of consolation to me.

During your last sojourn in this capital, you yourself, my dear friend, expressed your approval of these compositions. Your good opinion encourages me to offer them to you and leads me to hope that you will not consider them wholly unworthy of your favor. Please, then, receive them kindly and be to them a father, guide and friend. From this moment, I give to you all my rights over them. I beg of you to be indulgent toward those faults that may have escaped a father's partial eye, and despite them, continue your generous friendship they so highly appreciate. Meanwhile, I remain with all my heart, your dear friend, your most sincere friend,

W. A. Mozart
Vienna, 1st September 1785

Michael Haydn [younger brother of Franz Joseph] was supposed to compose duets for violin and viola on the highest orders [i.e., for the Archbishop]. But he was unable to deliver them on time, because he fell ill and was incapable of working for a longer period than he had expected. Because of this delay, he was threatened with cancellation of his salary.... Mozart, who visited Haydn every day, learned of this, sat down and wrote for his distressed friend with such uninterrupted speed that the duets were finished in a matter of days and could be delivered a few days later under Michael Haydn's name.

—GEORG NICOLAUS NISSEN, second husband of Constanze Mozart, who wrote with her an early biography of Mozart, published in Leipzig in 1828

In a famous meeting in Vienna, in the spring of 1787, the sixteen-year-old Beethoven came to play before Mozart. When he heard Beethoven's im-

provisations on a theme from *The Marriage of Figaro*, Mozart said, *"Keep your eye on him; he'll make the world talk of him one day."*

At an Augarten concert the two pianists Cramer and Beethoven were walking together and heard a performance of Mozart's pianoforte Concerto in C minor (K. 491). Beethoven suddenly stood still and, directing his companion's attention to the exceedingly simple, but equally beautiful motiv which is first introduced towards the end of the piece, exclaimed: "Cramer, Cramer! we shall never be able to do anything like that!" As the theme was repeated and wrought up to the climax, Beethoven, swaying his body to and fro, marked the time and in every possible manner manifested a delight rising to enthusiasm.

—A. W. Thayer, *The Life of Beethoven*

What a picture of a better world you have given us, Mozart! —Franz Schubert

Schubert's very successful statue in Stadt-Park doesn't seem to me a definite obstacle against the quintuple-monument [of Gluck, Haydn, Mozart, Beethoven, and Schubert—an idea Liszt had earlier proposed]: the chief difficulty rests in the composition of the group. To my way of thinking, the place in the center belongs to Mozart, due to the universality of his genius.　　　　　　　—FRANZ LISZT, in a letter to Marie zu Sayn-Wittgenstein, December 10, 1872

Does it not seem as if Mozart's works become fresher and fresher the oftener we hear them?
　　　　　　　　—ROBERT SCHUMANN

He asked me what I thought of the worthy Mozart and all his sins. I replied, however, that I should be only too happy to renounce all my virtues in exchange for Mozart's sins.
　　　　　　　　—FELIX MENDELSSOHN, *Letters*

If we cannot write with the beauty of Mozart, let us at least try to write with his purity.

> —JOHANNES BRAHMS, in a
> letter to Antonín Dvořák

The Germans have always been at all times the greatest harmonists, and the Italians the greatest melodists. But from the moment that the North produced a Mozart, we of the South were beaten on our own ground, because this man rises above all nations, uniting in himself the charm of Italian melody and all the profundity of German harmony. . . . [He is] the only musician who had as much knowledge as genius, and as much genius as knowledge.

> —GIOACCHINO ROSSINI

Asked which was his favorite amongst the great masters, Rossini said, "Beethoven I take twice a week, Haydn four times, and Mozart every day."

> —HERBERT WEINSTOCK, *Rossini*

Before Mozart, all my ambition turns to despair.
—CHARLES-FRANÇOIS GOUNOD

There are two kinds of genius: natural genius and rational genius. Though I admire the latter immensely, I will not hide the fact that the former has all my sympathies. Yes, I have the courage to prefer Raphael to Michelangelo, Mozart to Beethoven, and Rossini to Meyerbeer.
—GEORGES BIZET,
December 31, 1858

The marvellous beauty of his quartets and quintets, and of some of his sonatas, first converted me to this celestial genius, whom thenceforth I worshipped.
—HECTOR BERLIOZ, *Memoirs*

He [Offenbach] owes something to those French models (Philidor and Monsigny), but more to his idol Mozart; Rossini once affectionately called Jacques "the Mozart of the Champs-Elysées."
—ALEXANDER FARIS,
Jacques Offenbach

But for music to rise by virtue of its own power to the pitch of great comedy without ceasing to be in itself a complete and perfectly pure art, we must wait for Mozart to appear. His music is no longer like that of the French masters, a simple adaptation of music to words. His music is, by itself, superiorly organized; where Grétry puts only words to music, Mozart sees a situation which he forces himself to set to music envisaged as absolute art.

—PAUL DUKAS, *Comedy in Music*

Mozart encompasses the entire domain of musical creation, but I've got only the keyboard in my poor head.

—FRÉDÉRIC CHOPIN, letter to Delphine Potocka

A genius naturally can do without taste; for example, Beethoven. But Mozart, his equal in genius, has, in addition, the most delicate taste.

—CLAUDE DEBUSSY, in *Musician of France,* by V. I. Sercoff

Beauty must appeal to the senses, must provide us with immediate enjoyment, must impress us or insinuate itself into us without any effort on our own part. Take Leonardo da Vinci; take Mozart: these are the great artists. —CLAUDE DEBUSSY, in *The Theories of Claude Debussy, Musicien Française,* by Leon Vallas

What gives Bach and Mozart a place apart is that these two great expressive composers never sacrificed form to expression. As high as their expression may soar, their musical form remains supreme and all-efficient. —CAMILLE SAINT-SAËNS

Music in its flexibility offers inexhaustible resources. Give Mozart a fairy tale, and he creates without effort an immortal masterpiece.

—CAMILLE SAINT-SAËNS,
Portraits and Souvenirs,
1899

From Your Wisdom 61

If a man tells me he likes Mozart, I know in advance that he is a bad musician.
—FREDERICK DELIUS

Mozart remains the greatest prodigy in musical history, but he was brought up in a fine tradition—in opera, as well as in other music.
—GUSTAVE HOLST, *The Heritage of Music*

I believe in God, Mozart and Beethoven.
—RICHARD WAGNER

The most tremendous genius raised Mozart above all masters, in all centuries and in all the arts.
—RICHARD WAGNER

62 Mozartiana

"What kind of face would Bach, Handel, Haydn and Mozart make after hearing an opera by Wagner?" I shall not attempt to answer for the first three, but it is safe to say that Mozart, the universal genius whose mind was free from Philistinism and one-sidedness, would not only open his eyes wide, but would be as delighted as a child with all the new acquisitions in the departments of drama and orchestra. In this light must Mozart be viewed. . . . Where he is greatest, he embraces all times.

In Bach, Beethoven and Wagner we admire principally the depth and energy of the human mind; in Mozart, the divine instinct.

—EDVARD GRIEG, "Mozart and Wagner"

The masses have now arrived at R. Wagner—he deserves it!! They only respect the earlier masters—Bach, Beethoven, Mozart—because it would be a scandal if they didn't. But I wouldn't like to look into the souls of those people who applaud a Bach concerto, a late Beethoven quartet or even a Mozart aria or minuet with such enthusiasm, for fear of seeing the deadly boredom there.

—ALBAN BERG, in *Berg,* by
Willi Reich

The Mozart, Schubert and Chopin she [Yesipova, the great Russian pianist and teacher] insisted on my playing didn't seem to appeal to me. I was too preoccupied by the search for a new harmonic idiom to understand how anyone could waste his time over Mozart. . . . Nothing but 1, 4, and 5!

—SERGEI PROKOFIEV,
in *Prokofiev,* by Lawrence
and Elisabeth Hanson

Together with the puzzle, he gives you the solution.
—FERRUCCIO BUSONI

You say that my worship for Mozart is quite contrary to my musical nature. But perhaps it is just because—being a child of my day—I feel broken and spiritually out of joint, that I find consolation and rest in Mozart's music, wherein he gives expression to that joy of life which was part of his sane and wholesome temperament. —PYOTR ILICH TCHAIKOVSKY, in a letter to Nadejda von Meck

Certainly to occupy himself directly with the music of Mozart was for Strauss a major incentive, for his was no superficial devotion. He was once asked to write a preface for a book on "Mozart and Munich" but actually replied, "I cannot write about Mozart, I can only worship him." He took every opportunity when conducting to include a Mozart symphony in his programs, and in the great E flat and G minor Symphonies was in the habit of returning a second time to the

Trios after the *Menuetto da capo* because "such music should be heard more than once."

—NORMAN DEL MAR,
Richard Strauss

My teachers were primarily Bach and Mozart—and secondarily Beethoven, Brahms and Wagner.

—ARNOLD SCHOENBERG

Every composer should know the last seven symphonies of Mozart by heart.

—BÉLA BARTÓK

I like Mozart best when I have the sensation I am watching him think; one takes delight in watching him carefully choose orchestral timbres, or in following the melodic line as it takes flight from the end of his pen. Mozart tapped the source from which all music flows, expressing himself with a spontaneity and refinement and breathtaking rightness.

—AARON COPLAND

The "fun" in a Mozart symphony is not entirely unlike that of a baseball game. In baseball, all plays are severely within the rules; and to make certain that the rules are kept, umpires stand right on the field.

The composers of the hundred or more years preceding the overlap of the Chopin-Schumann-Wagner romantic period derived their main excitement, their top spiritual exaltation, from the masterly way in which they could knock home runs or move and skip about inside these binding, limiting classic rules.

Mozart's mastery was so superb, so utterly top-notch, that Mozart fans experienced exactly the same sensation which a modern baseball audience might feel today should its hometown team be blindfolded and still win hands down against a super-excellent non-blindfolded visiting team.

—GEORGE ANTHEIL, "Bad Boy of Music," in *Composers on Music*

The tendency today is to try and show that artists are just as "bad" as you and I, the only difference being that God, for some divine caprice, has given them a mysterious talent that, however, they hardly deserve. Those people do not realize that the Platonic vision of beauty that the artist is privileged to receive is nothing more than a glimpse that then becomes a tormenting memory he must try to recapture. This search for remembered perfection requires hard work, patience, intelligence and complete dedication.

Mozart rarely abandons his search and more often than not, with blinding intelligence and wisdom, he re-creates his remembered vision of beauty in all its perfection. Be it a lesson to the lazy artists of today, who peddle their onanistic games as works of art. No great composer will again appear among us until the young are taught that being a genius is not enough. —GIAN CARLO MENOTTI

68 Mozartiana

Responding to a *New York Times* questionnaire to musicians as to which composers they regard as underrated:

Mozart—since the highest rave is a gross understatement.
                              —PETER SCHICKELE
                              ("P. D. Q. Bach")

Bravo!

COUNTESS: Bravo! What a beautiful voice! I didn't know you sang so well.

SUSANNA: Oh, I must say, everything he does, he does well.

I like it more than any other music. He is number one!
—VLADIMIR HOROWITZ

Mozart's music is particularly difficult to perform. His admirable clarity exacts absolute cleanness; the slightest mistake in it stands out like black on white. As I heard Saint-Saëns say lately: "It is music in which all the notes must be heard." Essentially simple, natural, it demands a simple, natural expression

71

as well; in other words, that to which its interpreters, even the best intentioned, have least accustomed us.

—Gabriel Fauré

The simpler you do Mozart—which is to say, match the look of the opera to its sound—the better off you are.

—Beverly Sills, *Beverly*

The key to singing Mozart is simplicity. You should follow your instincts and stick to the emotional truthfulness that fills every page.

—Frederica von Stade

Throughout my career, Mozart has played a major part. Living with his music and performing it has made me realize that it is not only some of the greatest music ever written for the voice, but some of the most difficult. The real challenge comes in making it seem perfectly natural, almost like speech, so that nothing stands in the way of the drama.

—SAMUEL RAMEY

On the whole, Mozart's writing is very violinistic, but it is never easy. . . . You must play the music as written without adding any outside interpretation. The pieces that look, or even sound, easy, are the really hard ones. There must be sentiment without sentimentality. It must sound direct, the way a child is before growing too old.

—JASCHA HEIFETZ

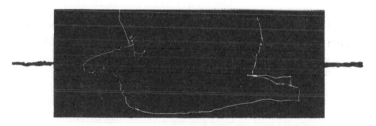

Mozart was a bad composer who died too late rather than too early.　—GLENN GOULD, in *Glenn Gould: A Life and Variations,* by Otto Friedrich

Mozart shows a creative power of such magnitude . . . that one can virtually say that he tossed out of himself one great masterpiece after another.

—CLAUDIO ARRAU,
Conversations with Arrau

[Countess Thun] told me she would venture her life that what I have written cannot fail to please. But on this point I pay no attention whatsoever to anybody's praise or blame—I simply follow my own feelings.

—MOZART, in a letter to
his father, 1781

We are told of Mozart's purity and of the simplicity of a Haydn or of a Couperin. But simplicity does not mean poverty, indigence and ignorance! When we say "the purity of Mozart," we are thinking of the impeccable tracing of his engraving tool, of his writing clear as crystal, but we are not then thinking of what his music expresses. Even when laden with amorous voluptuousness, Mozart's music remains pure.

... The works of Mozart may be easy to read, but they are very difficult to interpret. The least speck of dust spoils them. They are clear, transparent, and joyful as a spring, and not like those muddy pools which seem deep only because the bottom cannot be seen. —WANDA LANDOWSKA, *Landowska on Music*

Chopin's studies are lovely pieces, perfect pieces, but I simply can't spend time on them. I believe I know these pieces; but playing a Mozart sonata, I am not sure that I know it inside and out. Therefore I can spend endless time on it.

—ARTUR SCHNABEL, *My Life and Music*

When I was very young—a teenager—I was only enthusiastic for the great pathos and the big emotions, and Mozart seemed to me at that time too quiet, too tranquil. It needs some maturity to understand the depth of emotion which speaks in Mozart's seeming tranquillity and measure. I conducted very early the E-flat Symphony and the "Jupiter." Very immature and I'm sure it was absolutely not good. I was, I think, fifty when, for the first time, I was audacious enough to perform the G minor. I had such a feeling of responsibility. And I wondered at all the young conductors, who, without any qualms, just went ahead and conducted all these works which asked for such depth of feeling and such maturity of technique.

—Bruno Walter

I never heard so much content in so short a period.

—Pinchas Zukerman

Every "happy" musical idea of Mozart contains some thread of sadness; and every "sad" idea bears some measure of hope. This could be a partial clue, at least, to the *humanity* we sense in him. He understands, as we do, that joy is not unending, ultimately; and he knows that longing always contains some vision of that for which we long. . . . Could it be that in Mozart we hear a lucid expression, therefore, of what we most covet for ourselves?

—RICHARD WESTENBURG

Most of Mozart's music is dull.

—MARIA CALLAS, in *Maria Callas,* by Ariana Stassinopoulos

Mozart is usually sung with too much delicacy, as though the singer were on tiptoes, when his music should be performed with the same frankness and bel

canto approach one would use in *Il Trovatore,* for
example. Mozart, after all, was a master of bel canto
. . . so sing Mozart as though he were Verdi.

—MARIA CALLAS, in *Callas at
Juilliard*

You've got your diet all wrong. You've got to learn
Mozart before you try Verdi. Put the milk before the
meat. —RICHARD TUCKER

Art must be easy or impossible. Why does everything
Mozart wrote seem so simple? The way to this simplicity is hard labor but it must never seem like labor.

—ARTHUR RUBINSTEIN,
My Many Years

For one thing, he'll never hurt your voice. I'm young and I like how Mozart feels in the throat.

—MARGARET PRICE

The Queen of the Night [in *The Magic Flute*] is the most boring, pointless role I ever sang. [She] sings an aria in Scene i, Act I and sings another aria in Scene iii of Act II. Between arias, you sit backstage for at least an hour and a half.

The only redeeming feature of the role is its difficulty. At any given time only four or five sopranos in the world are able to sing the Queen of the Night. How high is a high F? *Very* high. In addition to those five high F's, the Queen's two arias contain some rather difficult coloratura passages. And you can't be a pipsqueak soprano, because the only bird the character resembles is a ravenous vulture. You've really got to be able to sock those notes out there. . . .

Because so few sopranos can sing the Queen of the Night, you can write your own ticket and live forever on that role. As soon as you perform it successfully a couple of times, you get an instant reputation. . . . The highest fees I ever received were not for my Rosalindas, Violettas and other roles, but for the Queen of the Night.   —BEVERLY SILLS, *Beverly*

The initial carelessness with which I treated the A major was due largely to my vanity—I was eager to get on to Beethoven, but the moment I surmounted that superficial attitude and immersed myself in the music, I discovered a greater affinity with Mozart than with any other composer.

. . . Mozart was able, because of the rigid conventions of his age, to pour his very genuine feelings into vessels the sheer elegance of which restrained their contents. He thus resolved his emotions on a level that transformed them into moods uncontaminated by mortal anguish . . . enabling Mozart to express the "angelic anguish" that is so peculiarly his own.

—YEHUDI MENUHIN, in *Menuhin,*
by Robert Magidoff

As a director, my definition of paradise would be to be perpetually rehearsing Mozart's operas.

—PETER HALL

Much as I love symphonic music, I think I will feel more at home conducting opera. . . . I would certainly love to do *Don Giovanni*—but then, what conductor would not?

—PLÁCIDO DOMINGO, *My First
Forty Years*

Years later, Toscanini said to me quite bluntly that he did not have a very comfortable feeling with Mozart and that Haydn was closer to him, because he could spot here and there the human hand of imperfection, while the infallibility of Mozart seemed awesome and superhuman. —ERICH LEINSDORF, *Cadenza*

Mozart makes you believe in God—much more than going to church—because it cannot be by chance that such a phenomenon arrives into this world and then passes after thirty-six years, leaving behind such an unbounded number of unparalleled masterpieces.
—GEORG SOLTI

Designing an opera by Mozart is like doing something for God—it's a labor of love.
—MAURICE SENDAK

In my dreams of Heaven, I always see the great Masters gathered in a huge hall in which they all reside. Only Mozart has his own suite.

—VICTOR BORGE

Spoken with Authority

ARTISTS AND CRITICS ON MOZART

DON ALFONSO: My hair is already gray. I speak with authority—but let's finish this argument.

Why does one continue to be preoccupied with Mozart? Here . . . we run into the question of why this music and its heritage interests not only scholars on the one hand, popular writers on the other, and the initiates (sometimes a combination of all three), but also why everyone with some musical receptivity is aware of the Phenomenon of Mozart. Why do people continue to be fascinated by this universal treasure? He has never yet been fathomed. . . . How can such a disproportionately large number of people have a definite, and unusually positive relationship to him?
—WOLFGANG HILDESHEIMER,
Mozart

Mozart's music is the mysterious language of a distant spiritual kingdom, whose marvellous accents echo in our inner being and arouse a higher, intensive life.

—E. T. A. HOFFMANN,
*Der Dichter und der
Komponist*

What else is genius than that productive power through which deeds arise, worthy of standing in the presence of God and Nature, and which, for this reason, bear results that are lasting? All the best creations of Mozart are of this class; within them there is a generative force which is transplanted from generation to generation, and is not likely soon to be exhausted.   —JOHANN WOLFGANG
VON GOETHE

Mozart's joy: a joy that you recognize to be lasting. Schumann's joy is feverish, as if it came between two sobs. Mozart's joy is made of serenity, and a phrase of his music is like a calm thought; his simplicity is merely purity. It is a crystalline thing in which all the emotions play a role, but as if already celestially transposed. "Moderation consists in feeling emotions as the angels do." (Joubert) To understand that remark completely you must think of Mozart.

—ANDRÉ GIDE, *Journals*

The straining after the basc excitement of the senses, after so-called beauty, shattered the nerves of the Italians: let us remain German! Even Mozart's relation to music—Wagner spoke this word of comfort to us—was at bottom frivolous.

—FRIEDRICH NIETZSCHE,
A Musician's Problem

Those fine minds I scandalize so have taken their time, I believe, in coming to understand Mozart's tragic quality. At one time they granted [him] no importance. . . . Art should inspire an erection in the soul. . . . Mozart must have had a charming and cruel soul, filled with grace and vitality.

—JEAN COCTEAU, *Past Tense*

A blind adoration of everything he wrote, even in his earlier years, has prevented a true appreciation of the unique qualities of Mozart's mature compositions. The layman is led to believe that all of Mozart is somehow divine and above any criticism, and with this unrealistic approach he cannot (or, if one will, dare not) differentiate between what is beautiful and what is sublime, between what is good Mozart and what is great Mozart. The pity of this uncritical attitude is that Mozart's real achievements—far greater

than many of his most ardent admirers realize—are
simply taken for granted.

—H. C. ROBBINS LANDON,
The Mozart Companion

Marcel Proust . . . wrote in Antoinette Fauré's con-
fession-album: "Favorite composers, Gounod and
Mozart." —GEORGE PAINTER, *Proust: The
Early Years*

Mozart is happiness before it has gotten defined.
—ARTHUR MILLER

An evening spent at a theater was a rare event. It had
to be something of special interest to him [Freud],
such as a performance of a Shakespeare play or a
Mozart opera, before he could tear himself from his
work. —ERNEST JONES, *The Life and
Work of Sigmund Freud*

GEORGE BERNARD SHAW
on Mozart:

From Shakespeare and Swift I learned to write but from Mozart I got my ideas.

And then you must modulate. Unless you can produce in speaking exactly the same effect Mozart produces when he stops in C and then begins again in A-flat, you can't play Shakespeare.

—LETTER TO MRS. PATRICK
CAMPBELL, 1921

Mozart was the greatest of all musicians. He taught me how to say profound things and at the same time remain flippant and lively.

With Mozart you are safe from inebriety. Hurry, excitement, eagerness, loss of consideration, are to him purely comic or vicious states of mind. . . . Give me the artist who breathes the true Parnassian air like a native and goes about his work as a common man goes about his ordinary business. Mozart did so; and that is why I like him. Even if I did not, I should pretend to; for a taste for his music is a mark of caste among musicians, and should be worn like a tall hat by the amateur who wishes to pass for a true Brahmin.

The extent and range of Mozart's genius are so vast and so bewildering that any concise summing-up of his achievement must risk being trite. He took the musical small-change of his day, learned from childhood in the courts of Europe, and transformed it into a mint of gold. . . . In his operas he not only displayed hitherto unequalled dramatic feeling, but widened the boundaries of the singer's art, and with his amazing insight into human nature created characters on the stage . . . the equal of Shakespeare's. Not by revolutionary deliverance, by the natural superiority of the music he wrote, he changed the course of the symphony, the piano concerto, the string quartet, the sonata, and much more besides. "Mozart is music," one critic said, and most composers since 1791 have agreed. —MICHAEL KENNEDY, *The Oxford Dictionary of Music*

Dearest B.B.,
Robert and I are this moment back from three days of (comparatively) riotous living in Nice, where we went after Landowska's departure, alléchés by a Mozart festival in the shape of several of M.'s operas with Lotte Schoene and a Viennese troupe. . . . We had two delicious evenings with *Die Entführung* and *Figaro,* the latter simply *ravishing."*

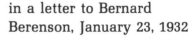

—EDITH WHARTON, in a letter to Bernard Berenson, January 23, 1932

All in all, Mozart's music is the voice of an aristocratic age that had not heard the Bastille fall, and a Catholic culture undisturbed in its faith, free to enjoy

the charms of life without the restless search to find new content for an emptied dream. . . . It is, by and large, serene music, touched now and then by suffering and anger, but raising neither a humble prayer nor a Promethean challenge to the gods. Mozart began his works in childhood, and a childlike quality lurked in his compositions until it dawned upon him that the Requiem which he was writing for a stranger was his own. —WILL AND ARIEL DURANT,
Rousseau and Revolution

He touched no problem without solving it to perfection. —DONALD TOVEY, *Essays in Musical Analysis*

Mozart's incomparability lies in the absolute nature of his achievements; the best of [his works] cannot be even slightly rewritten without diminishment. Of course, great art always attests to the existence of absolutes; that is why the greatest offers the largest comfort—even as, temporarily, it can also induce the largest despair. —PETER SHAFFER, in *Opera Anecdotes,* by Ethan Mordden

I often tell my students, when they are depressed by the world, that there are two things that make my life worth living, Mozart and quantum mechanics. —VICTOR F. WEISSKOPF, *The Privilege of Being a Physicist*

Mozart is the greatest composer of all. Beethoven "created" his music, but the music of Mozart is of such purity and beauty that one feels he merely "found" it—that it has always existed as part of the inner beauty of the universe waiting to be revealed. —ALBERT EINSTEIN

The perfected works of a Racine or a Mozart do not at first make as deep an impression as those of geniuses who are more unpolished. The salient parts of these last seem all the more striking because other parts nearby are more neutral, or downright bad.

. . . Mozart might say of himself, though he would have said it in less swollen terms: "Je suis maître de moi, comme de l'univers." Mounted on the chariot of his improvisation, and like Apollo at the zenith of his course . . . it is with a firm hand that he holds the reins of his racers as he sheds light everywhere.

—EUGÈNE DELACROIX, *Journals*

I do not have the gift, a gift I would dearly love to possess, of finding words to describe music; my models of such a gift would be Plato and Nietzsche. But, throughout my life, Mozart has been as close to the simple, sensuous experience of the beautiful as I have ever encountered. That experience has been an antidote to all the seductions of nihilism present in our world. This is heightened by the fact that Mozart's own life is one that could so easily have led another to despair. It has happened more than once that a student ignorant of classical music has come to my home, heard a bit of Mozart in the background, asked, "What is that?" and been launched on a voyage of musical discovery.

Most of all I adore Mozart's capacity to be both deep and rational, a combination often said to be impossible. As Rossini recognized, no composer was as witty as Mozart.   —ALLAN BLOOM

If we want to grasp the real greatness of Mozart and if we want to understand the profound secret of the power of redemption of his music, we must always remember that this man suffered the pains and agonies of a noble soul frustrated and contemptuously humiliated. The inexhaustible capacity for love which was the dominant trait in his nature prevented the sufferings from striking the dominant tone in his works. —PAUL HENRY LANG, *Music in Western Civilization*

Mozart was a prodigious artist whose work at each stage of his life continues to delight and inspire. I never tire of it. —BILL BRADLEY

Had Mozart (or for that matter Beethoven) been living today, I doubt very much whether he would have given us that wonderful flood of great music that he did. A genius like him would very soon have been seduced financially either by Hollywood to write film-music or by television to show off before millions or by the stage to write piffling musical comedies. This has happened to virtually every promising musical talent since Stravinsky, with the possible exception of Britten.

For this reason, I don't believe the world is ever going to see the likes of Bach or Mozart or Beethoven or Schubert or Brahms or Sibelius again, not of course that they happen very often anyway. We must be thankful for what we've got.

—ROALD DAHL

The science of harmony may eventually explore the obscurest and remotest frontiers of music; yet at the end of each road which leads to new knowledge, the explorers will be amazed to discover that Mozart has been there before them. Thus, in the technical, purely mechanical aspect of his art, Mozart can never be surpassed; and any composer who attempted to outdo him on this count would be like a painter who tried to outdo Titian in the effectiveness of realism of his coloring, or like a dramatist who tried to better Racine in the purity of his verse or in the delicacy of his expression.

As to the spiritual qualities of Mozart's music, the tempest-wind of his impetuous genius will never lack the power to sweep away the dreaming, contemplative spirits of this world, nor fill their world with sad and haunting visions. Sometimes the impact of his music is so immediate that the vision in the mind remains blurred and incomplete, while the *soul* seems to be directly invaded, drenched, as it were, in wave upon wave of melancholy.

—STENDHAL, *Life of Rossini*

You could put all my musicology into the *o* in *into*, but I write and listen to things as intently as I can, and Mozart's combination of high formality and playfulness delights me as no other composition in any medium does. Homer is cruel, Michelangelo isn't funny, Shakespeare is uneven, Beethoven is German, Faulkner goes overboard and Ray Charles has let his band get too big, but the pleasures of Mozart are unqualifiable, so far as I can tell. His rigorous loveliness, cleanly busy, voluptuously fine, heartens my belief in a thoroughly, joyfully responsible free hand. Hot dickety.   —ROY BLOUNT, JR.

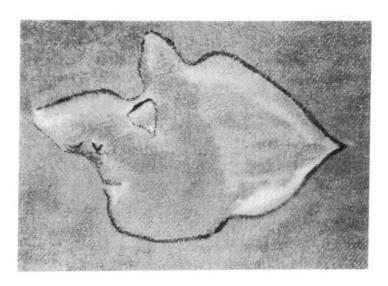

Hear the Musicians

INSTRUMENTAL WORKS

DON GIOVANNI: Now cheer up, both of you. Do you hear the musicians? Come along with me.

This incident, related by Andreas Schachtner, occurred when Mozart was four years old.

PAPA: What are you doing?
MOZART: *Writing a clavier concerto; I'm almost done.*
PAPA: Show it to me.
MOZART: *It is not finished yet.*
PAPA: Never mind, let me see it.

His father took it and showed me a scribble of notes, most of it written over blots which had been rubbed out. Little Wolfgang, out of ignorance, had dipped his pen to the bottom of the inkwell; the result was a blot, but he at once made his decision, passed the back of his hand over it, smeared it over, and started merrily writing it again. We laughed at first at what seemed to be just nonsense, but the father then gave heed to the important part, the notes and composition, and he remained for a long time motionless with his attention fixed on the sheet. Finally he let fall some tears— tears of admiration and joy. "See, Herr Schachtner," he said, "how correct and regular everything is; only it isn't playable; it's so terribly hard that no one could perform it." *"That's just why it's a concerto,"* interrupted little Wolfgang. *"One must practice it until one succeeds."*   —ANDREAS SCHACHTNER, in a letter to Wolfgang's sister Nannerl, 1760

Mozart visited England when he was barely seven years old, and was received kindly by King George III (who twelve years later would find himself at war in the American colonies). At one court performance, little Wolfgang stood before the organ—and between the legs of Johann Christian Bach, the eleventh son of Johann Sebastian. At certain moments in the piece, Bach would stop playing and Wolfgang would continue; then Mozart would pause and Bach resume. The two players alternated with such fluidity that no one guessed that there were two organists in the performance.

I herewith hand over the Mozart theme together with its history. This virtuoso honoured the city of Prague with a visit in June 1787, in order to make the acquaintance of the musicians of this capital. . . . He came to the Strahov Church one afternoon with Frau von Duschek, and expressed his desire to hear the organ . . . then he conceived the desire to play the organ himself. He mounted the console and played splendid chords, *pleno choro,* for some four minutes. He now began a four-part fugue theme, which was the harder to perform in that it and its counter-subject consisted largely of mordents, which are exceptionally hard to perform on an organ with such heavy action. I concentrated on the development of the theme, but Father Lohelius disturbed me with questions . . . so that I could not tell how he modulated so swiftly into D sharp major. Wanting to conclude in this key, he set about making a pedal-point. Holding a B flat in the bass as his dominant, he attacked the two upmost staves of the keyboard with both hands, gathering up so many notes and piling suspensions and resolutions on one another to such an extent that there he was playing in B major as beautifully as if it had been an F sharp that he was holding as pedal. . . . Then he developed the theme of a fugue from Brixi's Requiem in C minor in quite a different manner, but so artistically, that we stood there as if made of stone.

—NORBERT IGNAZ LOEHMANN,
to Franz Niemetschek, first
biographer of Mozart,
May 1, 1818

To my mind, the organ is the king of instruments.
—MOZART

During his sojourn in Leipzig in 1789, Mozart visited the Thomas-Kirche and heard the choir perform Johann Sebastian Bach's motet, *Singet dem Herrn ein neues Lied,* led by Cantor Doles, a former pupil of Bach's:

The chorus had hardly sung a few measures when Mozart exclaimed, *"What is this?"* and now all his soul seemed to be in his ears. And when the singing was over, he declared, full of joy, *"That, decidedly, is something from which one may learn!"* He was told that this school, at which Sebastian Bach had been cantor, possessed a complete collection of his motets and preserved them as a kind of sacred relic. *"That is right, that is good,"* he exclaimed, *"show them to me."* But no one had scores of these vocal compositions, so he asked for the parts. And now it was a joy for the quiet observer to see Mozart sit, all intensity, distributing the parts around him, holding some in his hands, putting others on his knees and the chairs around him, and not rising until he had scanned everything of Bach that was there.

Later that same day Mozart went to the organ:

[He] improvised magnificently on every theme given. . . . Doles was wholly delighted with Mozart's playing and believed old Sebastian Bach, his teacher, had risen from the grave.

—FRIEDRICH ROCHLITZ, in a
Leipzig music periodical, 1801

. . . at the end, a Mozart symphony which delighted me. My fatigue and the heat were excessive; but I had an experience there which never happened to me before; it was that the last piece seemed not only ravishing in every respect but that, apparently, it caused my fatigue to disappear while I was listening. That perfection, that completeness, those delicate shadings, all that must be the despair of musicians who have any soul and any taste.

—Eugène Delacroix, *Journals*

Melody became the very element of the Symphony of song-abundant and song-glad Mozart. He breathed into his instruments the passionate breath of *Human Voice,* that voice toward which his genius bent with overmastering love. He led the stanchless stream of teeming harmony into the very heart of melody; to

give it that depth of feeling and fervour that forms the exhaustless source of human utterance within the inmost chambers of the heart. Whilst, in his symphonies he lifted up the "singing" power of instrumental music to such a height that it was now enabled, not only to embrace the mirth and inward content which it had learnt from Haydn, but the whole depth of endless heart's desire. —RICHARD WAGNER,
Prose Works

We know the Haffner symphony (K. 385) today in the form in which Mozart himself performed it in Vienna on 23 March 1783, after adding flutes and clarinets. He had lost all recollection of it by the time Leopold sent it back to him (letter of 15 February 1783); *"My new Haffner symphony has positively amazed me, for I had forgotten every single note of it."*

—ALFRED EINSTEIN, *Mozart: His Character, His Work*

My love of Mozart, and affinity for his music, is I suppose best documented by my having chosen to write my senior paper in music history on the Haffner Symphony. I can't remember what I said, but for me at the time, it epitomized the capacity of Wolfgang Amadeus Mozart to communicate sadness gaily. And I remember the personal hurt I experienced on reading the obituary of Arthur Sulzberger—he had specified that no Mozart should be played at his funeral service. I remember the indignation that welled up in me, as though defending Mozart would need to be an eternal commitment. . . . It is hardly that, in an epoch in which the most conspicuous music festival in the Western world is called Mostly Mozart. He is ours to cherish, perpetually.

—WILLIAM F. BUCKLEY

The Andante in C minor (of the Sinfonia Concertante in E Flat Major, K. 364) is a movement of such profound feeling that it has been suggested it was a Requiem for Mozart's dead mother. This is, I think, to misunderstand Mozart's creative process, which transformed human emotions through the prism of his genius and never portrayed them directly. Thus, for instance, the very first work he wrote after hearing of the death of his beloved father was the "Musikalischer Spass" ("A Musical Joke"), and so too he was able to compose the serene music of his last years though suffering from great hardship.

—ERIK SMITH, on the
Sinfonia Concertante

Although Haydn has the credit of having invented the symphonic form as we know it today, it was nonetheless Mozart who, in his "Paris" Symphony (D major, K. 297), written when he was twenty-two years of age, wrote the first incontestably genuine symphony to appear on the European scene. . . . It was always Mozart who was the first to create, in wholly satisfactory shape and detail, those musical forms which were not only a great achievement in themselves but which were the models for almost everything in the symphonic line written during the 100 years that followed. —THOMAS BEECHAM

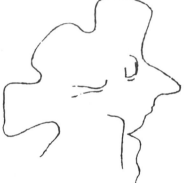

A week later came Elgar's lecture on Mozart's G minor symphony. He began the lecture: "Turning from a modern score to this small attenuated orchestra, a pitiful array of instruments, we may wonder how is it possible that a great art-work could be evolved from such sorry materials. . . . We have to marvel that with such a selection of instruments, a variety and contrast can be found sufficient to hold the attention for thirty minutes." This is the very symphony which had been the model of his own professional study almost thirty years earlier.

—Jerrold N. Moore,
Elgar: A Creative Life

What a piece! No amount of analysis or explanation can prepare one for the overwhelming surprise of its existence when it is actually heard in performance. It is hard to think of another work that so perfectly marries form and passion.

—Leonard Bernstein, on the
Symphony in G minor

The G minor symphony consists of eight remarkable measures . . . surrounded by a half-hour of banality.

—Glenn Gould, *The Glenn
Gould Reader*

Michael Bourges, a nineteenth-century music critic, wrote of the Jupiter Symphony:

In this work, despite its elegance, and despite the enormous facility of the writer, we find too many out-of-date formulas . . . too much aimless development, too many laborious technical procedures, especially in the finale. The skill of the performers can doubtless create illusions, but it could not prevent the adagio from being diffuse and dragging, nor the last movement from being cold and meaningless, despite its admirable construction—a perfect academic model. —GEORGES DE SAINT-FOIX,
The Symphonies of Mozart

Klee [in 1927] referred to Mozart's Jupiter Symphony as "the highest attainment in art," describing its finale as "the summit of all daring. This movement is decisive for all subsequent musical history."
—WILL GROHMANN, *Paul Klee*

Notice posted in the *Weiner Zeitung*, April 2, 5, and 9, 1788:

Three new quintets for two violins, two violas and cello which, beautifully and correctly written, I offer on subscription. The price is four ducats or eighteen gulden in Viennese currency. The subscriptions may be ordered daily from Herr Puchberg at Sallinz' business establishment in the High Market, where from the first of July on, the works themselves will be available. I request out-of-town music lovers to pay postage for delivery.

—Kappellmeister Mozart in the Service of His Majesty

I go back to the G Minor Quintet for comfort, sometimes when I am most desperate. The kind of consolation it affords is parallel to what Wordsworth's poetry gives me—helping me to bear myself in the despair of solitude. —HAROLD BLOOM

The Quintet in G minor for two violas tears your heart out. —ZUBIN MEHTA

The other three divertimenti (K. 247, 287, 334), however, which could be called simply string quartets with two obbligato horns, are among the purest, gayest, most satisfying, and most perfect that ever assumed musical form; and there are people who would trade a whole act of *Tannhäuser* or *Lohengrin* for one of those works, a lost paradise of music.
—ALFRED EINSTEIN, *Mozart:*
His Character, His Work

When I was in Rome, I saw a simple waltz by Mozart charm every singer, male and female, for almost four years. —JEAN-AUGUSTE-DOMINIQUE INGRES, *Notes on Music and Musicians*

Five violin concertos (K. 207, 211, 216, 218 and 219), his most notable contribution to this specific form, were composed in 1775, his nineteenth year. Taken, all in all, this series is an amazing performance. It will seem that nineteen is hardly the age for the production of earth-shaking masterpieces. In all truth, there have been greater wonders than these concertos known in the world, some of them productions of the mature Mozart. Yet many a reputable composer thrice his age would have fallen over his academic shoelaces for a chance to claim as his own the incredible fluency of musical speech, the rich-

ness of texture, and the sheer beauty of melodic line that pervades this music. —ABRAHAM VEINUS,
The Concerto

[Constanze] confirmed the truth of [Mozart's] writing the Quartet in D minor while she was in labor with their first child: several passages [are] indicative of her sufferings, especially the Minuet (a part which she sang to us). . . .

—VINCENT NOVELLO, after visiting
Constanze in 1829, in *A Mozart Pilgrimage*

I found myself utterly seduced by the passage in A minor that gives the concerto its nickname, "Turkish." How could my sense of humor have been so blunt as to miss this delightful episode which wandered over from [*The Abduction from the Seraglio*], startling the classical minuet with Turkish military buffoonery? or the ascending phrase that concludes the work on an inconclusive note, as if to pull a well-upholstered formula from under somnolent lords and ladies? or the gypsy elements that normally made my ears prick? Mozart, having won his way into my heart with Oriental tricks and enchanting burlesque, soon enthralled me by his least grace note.

—YEHUDI MENUHIN,
Unfinished Journey

The piano quartet K. 478 in G minor (1785) furnishes conclusive proof, more than any other single masterpiece of his, that Mozart's was the only truly omniscient ear of which we know.

—HANS KELLER, *The Mozart Companion*

MOZART, 1935

Poet, be seated at the piano.
Play the present, its hoo-hoo-hoo,
Its shoo-shoo-shoo, its ric-a-nic,
Its envious cachinnation.

If they throw stones upon the roof
While you practice arpeggios,
It is because they carry down the stairs
A body in rags.
Be seated at the piano.

That lucid souvenir of the past,
The divertimento;
That airy dream of the future,
The unclouded concerto . . .
The snow is falling.
Strike the piercing chord.

Be thou the voice,
Not you. Be thou, be thou
The voice of angry fear,
The voice of this besieging pain.

Be thou that wintry sound
As of the great wind howling,
By which sorrow is released,

Dismissed, absolved
In a starry placating.

We may return to Mozart.
He was young, and wc, we are old.
The snow is falling
And the streets are fully of cries.
Be seated, thou.
—WALLACE STEVENS

In the piano concertos there are pastoral, Arcadian
scenes of an indescribable poetry, and so apparently
simple that they are the very breath of inspiration
itself.　　　　　　　—SACHEVERELL SITWELL,
Mozart

We must never lose sight of the fact that the operas
and the pianoforte concertos are the works in which

we meet Mozart most closely . . . they are the ones which represent his individual personality most intimately and completely.

—Edward J. Dent, *Mozart's Operas: A Critical Study*

My first visit was to Mozart's house, where to my joy I found his parents had lived quite comfortably. When I saw the clavichord of this beloved master, I could not resist and played the beginning of the second movement of the A major concerto, which brought a tear to my eye. The tourists who filled the room felt, as I did, the presence of this genius and were wiping their eyes.

—Arthur Rubinstein, *My Many Years*

Here and there are things which only connoisseurs can appreciate, but I have seen to it that those less

knowledgeable must also be pleased without know-
ing why. —MOZART, about his piano
concertos K. 449, 450, 451

The sonatas of Mozart are unique; they are too easy
for children, and too difficult for artists.
—ARTUR SCHNABEL

Those who had the good fortune to hear Mozart play
the pianoforte were ecstatic in describing his *can-
tilena*, which seemed to issue from the throat of a
singer rather than from the keyboard of an instrument. —WANDA LANDOWSKA

The composer and pianist Muzio Clementi was considered by many to be Mozart's sole rival at the keyboard. In 1781, the Emperor Joseph arranged for a

competition of piano virtuosity between them. Mozart won, but not graciously. He reports:

He plays well, at least as far as the right hand goes. He has not an atom of taste or feeling; in fact, he is a mere mechanist. . . . Clementi is a charlatan, like all Italians! —MOZART, in a letter to his father

Clementi had kinder things to say. At first, he thought Mozart was "an individual whose elegant attire led me to take him for a royal valet-de-chambre." But later: "Until then, I had never heard anyone play with such divine grace and expression."

Pianists . . . peep out from every corner. To a man, and at all ages, they are occupied with what seems to be the central esthetic problem in music today: the cre-

ation of an acceptable style-convention for performing Mozart. —VIRGIL THOMSON, *Virgil
Thomson by Virgil Thomson*

It is time to cast aside this shibboleth of printer's ink
and paper and look the thing itself straight in the face.
It is a fact that Mozart's sonatas are compositions
entirely unworthy of the author of *The Magic Flute*,
or of any composer with pretensions to anything
beyond mediocrity. They are written in a style of
flashy harpsichord virtuosity such as Liszt never de-
scended to, even in those of his works at which so
many persons are accustomed to sneer.
—EDWARD MACDOWELL

*Wolfgang Amadeus Mozart takes pity on that Ass,
Ox and Fool, Leutgeb, here in Vienna, the 27th of
May, 1783.* —MOZART, the dedication
of the horn concerti

When the Salzburg horn player Ignaz
Leutgeb received the three horn concerti dedicated to him by Mozart, he
noticed that some of the score was
written in a bright blue ink—these
were the difficult moments in the
pieces, to which Mozart gleefully
added his commentary in the margins:
"What do you say to that, *Master
Leutgeb?!"*

I have often thought that Mozart, who wrote for so
many instruments, must have written a cello con-

certo. But nowhere is there any mention of it. . . . Why did Mozart think that in his day cello technique was not sufficiently developed?

—PABLO CASALS, *Conversations with Casals*

A critical review of the manner in which the concertos for wind instruments have come down to us is very instructive. It shows that Mozart wrote concertos for a definite instrument only at a definite time and always for a definite player or client. In so far as they were completed at all, the bassoon concertos were written for Dürnitz during the years 1774–5; and as Mozart never again had close relations with any other bassoon player . . . he never composed another bassoon concerto. The oboe Concerto K. 271 was commissioned by Ferlendis, and after 1777 Mozart did not write another until a new patron made his appearance at Vienna in 1783 . . . so far as we can tell the horn concertos were all written for Leutgeb. . . . Mozart began to occupy himself with writing for the

solo clarinet only when he found a satisfactory solo-
ist in Stadler. . . . He wrote not one horn concerto "on
spec," still less for publication, and not one of his
wind concertos was published in his lifetime. Nor
was it mood or inspiration that occasioned a composition, but demand, an opportunity to have a work
performed, someone's need of friendly assistance, or
a paid commission.

—FRIEDRICH BLUME,
"The Concertos," in
The Mozart Companion

At the age of twenty-two, Mozart was commissioned
by a wealthy amateur flautist, De Jean, to write three
short concerti and two quartets for the flute. But:

*It is not surprising that I have been unable to finish
them. . . . Certainly I could be scribbling all day, but
a composition of this kind goes out into the world,
and naturally I do not want to have cause to be
ashamed of my name on the title page. Moreover, you*

know that I become quite powerless whenever I am
obliged to write for an instrument that I cannot bear.

—MOZART, in a letter to his
father, February 24, 1778

We may assert, not only that no composer in the
genre before or after him ever even approximated the
quality of Mozart wind concerti, but also that his
treatment of the woodwinds has never been surpassed. They are combined with a precision that
never hardens into a pattern; pure melody and *canti-*
bile style are differentiated to achieve enormous sug-
gestivity in the instrumental timbre (think of their
role in the great piano concerti). Only two composers
ever matched him in this: Berlioz and Mahler.

—WOLFGANG HILDESHEIMER,
Mozart

One of the earliest [wind-band serenades] is also the
greatest—the Serenade for Thirteen Instruments in
B-flat (K. 361). . . . A leading expert on the subject,

Roger Hellyer, now considers that the Serenade was in fact . . . Mozart's wedding present to Constanze in 1782. (This, like Wagner's *Siegfried Idyll,* must constitute one of the greatest gifts of music ever made by a composer to his wife.)

—H. C. ROBBINS LANDON,
Mozart, The Golden Years

Mozart was the first to appreciate the true importance of the clarinet both in chamber music and in the orchestra. . . . He could not have found in Gluck's or even Haydn's earlier clarinet-writing anything like his own sense of the value of every part of the instrument's compass. . . .

In the E-flat symphony, Mozart compels himself to use the clarinets in all possible ways, because he does without oboes throughout the work. In the G minor symphony he at first did without clarinets, but he afterwards rewrote the oboe-parts, giving all their softer and less rustic utterances to the clarinets. . . . The whole orchestra is affected by these differences of scheme: and an intimate knowledge of these [scores] is the foundation of a fine sensibility toward the possibilities of modern orchestration.

—DONALD FRANCIS TOVEY,
Essays in Musical Analysis

Of his 1938 recording of Mozart's Clarinet Quintet:

I just plunged into it. I had a kind of jazz vibrato, but I just played. Later it struck me that I really would like to know what the hell I'm doing.

—BENNY GOODMAN, who then studied classical repertoire and in 1940 recorded Mozart's Clarinet Concerto

I have been told that a young would-be composer wrote to Mozart, asking advice as to how to compose a symphony. Mozart responded that a symphony was a complex and demanding musical form and that it would be better to start with something simpler. The young man protested, "But Herr Mozart, you wrote symphonies when you were younger than I am now." And Mozart replied, *"I never asked how."*

That is my favorite Mozart story.

—ISAAC ASIMOV

Now for the Serenade

THE OPERAS

DON GIOVANNI: These are the windows. . . . Now for the serenade.

Simply to hear anyone speak of an opera, or to be in the theatre, or to hear singing is enough to be almost beside myself! —MOZART, in a letter to his father, October 11, 1777

No composer—not Verdi, not Wagner, for all their greatness—had Mozart's gift for devising music so close to his characters, or for using music in its greatest variety to underscore the high points in his dramas. —ALAN RICH

Mozart wrote his first opera, *La finta simplice,* at the age of twelve, but the cabals of his rivals kept it off the Salzburg stage. The first operatic work of his to be performed, *Bastien and Bastienne,* was produced privately in 1768 at the Vienna home of the celebrated hypnotist Dr. Anton Mesmer (whose theories Mozart would later satirize in *Così Fan Tutte*); his first major opera to be fully staged was *Mitridate, King of Ponto* (K. 87), which had its premiere in Milan on December 26, 1770—when Mozart was fourteen.

Opera comes to me before everything else.
>   —MOZART, in a letter to his
>   father, August 17, 1782

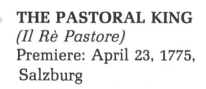

THE PASTORAL KING
(Il Rè Pastore)
Premiere: April 23, 1775,
Salzburg

Last night my opera was performed, and with such success that I cannot hope to describe to mamma the

*intense uproar. Applause and shouting after every
aria, and even between the opera and the ballet,
when the house is usually quiet, such applause! The
Court congratulated me and said such nice things.
. . . Adieu! A thousand kisses to Pimperl [the dog].
Your small composer.*

—MOZART, in a letter to
Nannerl, January 13, 1775

**IDOMENEO,
KING OF CRETE**
(Idomeneo, Rè di Creta)
Premiere: January 29,
1781, Munich

I recommend you to think when at work not only of
the musical but also of the unmusical public. You
know that for every ten connoisseurs, there are a
hundred ignoramuses! Do not neglect the so-called
popular. —LEOPOLD MOZART, in a letter
to his son about the
writing of *Idomeneo*

Now for the Serenade 133

Idomeneo was performed only twice in Mozart's lifetime and had long been neglected when Richard Strauss staged it in Vienna in 1931. The work did not reach the United States until August 4, 1947, in a Tanglewood production; it premiered at the Metropolitan Opera in 1982.

[In 1964] I sang the part of Idamante at Glyndebourne and fell in love with the entire opera. It has to be done [right] for people to realize how big and how important it is. . . . The acting is intense, extremely internal.

—LUCIANO PAVAROTTI, in
Opera News

[Electra], rising to the challenge of her wildly florid "D'Oreste, d'Ajace," went properly berserk, to the point of falling down in a grand seizure. . . . Probably she was as much undone by the aria's 33 A-flats and a couple of high C's as by jealousy and anger; but the effect was tremendous just the same.

—DONAL HENAHAN, in a review
in *The New York Times*,
1986

It is perhaps the most beautiful ensemble ever composed for the stage [of the Act III quartet, "Andrò, ramingo e solo"]. . . .

More than ever now, in these times of turmoil and confusion . . . we need the profound and noble sincerity of *Idomeneo* and the serene spirituality of *The Magic Flute.* —EDWARD J. DENT, *Mozart's Operas: A Critical Study*

THE ABDUCTION FROM THE SERAGLIO
(Die Entführung aus dem Serail) Premiere: July 16, 1782, Vienna

Herewith I enclose the original [score] and two word-books. Here and there, the trumpets and kettle-drums, flutes, clarinets and the Turkish music are missing, because I couldn't find paper with that many staves. They are written on extra sheets; I presume the copyist has lost them. . . . The first act (when I

*was taking it somewhere or other—I can't remember
where) fell in the mud; that's why it's dirty.*

> —MOZART, in a letter to his
> father, July 20, 1782

After the Vienna premiere—

> EMPEROR JOSEPH: Too fine for our ears,
> and an immense number of notes, my
> dear Mozart.
> MOZART: *Just as many notes, Your Maj-
> esty, as are required.*

*All the forte passages contain the Turkish music.
. . . I don't think they'll be able to sleep through it,
even if they haven't slept the night before.*

> —MOZART, in a letter to his
> father, about the overture to
> *Abduction,* September 26, 1781

While Mozart was in Berlin in 1789, *Die Entführung* was performed there once again. On the evening of the performance the sixteen-year-old Ludwig Tieck, an admirer of Mozart's work, spoke to a small, ordinary-looking man in a grey topcoat who was glancing over the music-desks in the orchestra while the auditorium was still empty. As they got into conversation, Tieck said how much he admired Mozart's operas. The stranger appeared interested, remarking that it was good of the young man to be fond of them. The theatre filled; the older man was called away, but Tieck felt some urge to discover his identity. He learnt he had spoken to the great composer himself. More than sixty years later he described this convincingly straightforward and moving incident. Mozart must have been touched, encouraged too, by such a youthful enthusiast.

—MICHAEL LEVEY, *The Life and Death of Mozart*

It was perhaps on that particular evening in Berlin that Mozart became enraged to hear how the orchestra was "improvising" on the score of his *Ab-*

duction. Rising from his seat, he rushed down the aisle toward the stage shouting, *"Verflucht, wollt Ihr D greifen!* (Will you play D natural, you rogues!)"

Mozart married Constanze Weber on August 4, 1782. He often jokingly called his marriage, which his father opposed, *Die Entführung aus dem Auge Gottes*—the abduction from Auge Gottes—Auge Gottes being the name of the Weber home.

We poor, common folk must not only take wives whom we love and who love us, but we may, can and want to take such because we are neither noble, well-born nor rich, but lowly, mean and poor. Hence we do not need rich wives, because our wealth dies with us, being in our heads. Of this wealth no man can rob us unless he cuts off our heads, in which case we should have need of nothing more.

—MOZART, in a letter to
his father

138 Mozartiana

Mozart's operas exist precariously at a moment of transition between old and new regimes in society and music. They begin from classical formality, but they are agitated by a romantic impetuosity of emotion.
—PETER CONRAD,
A Song of Love and Death

THE MARRIAGE OF FIGARO
(Le Nozze di Figaro)
Premiere: May 1, 1786, Vienna

I looked on with the greatest pleasure while all these people flew about in sheer delight to the music of my Figaro, *arranged for quadrilles and waltzes. For here they talk of nothing but* Figaro. *Nothing but* Figaro. *No opera is pulling in the crowds like* Figaro. *Nothing but* Figaro! *Certainly a great honor for me.*
—MOZART, in a letter to his father from Prague, 1787

There are no winners or losers in *Figaro,* only slightly bewildered people who cope with the game of life....

I turn the pages of any Mozart score and marvel. This genius defined the human condition in his music and we bravely try to squeeze his universe into the theater.

—JEAN-PIERRE PONNELLE,
director, 1985–86 production
at the Metropolitan Opera,
New York

The opera bored me.

—COUNT KARL ZINZENDORF, 1786

Of all the performers in this opera at that time, only one survives—myself. It was allowed that never was an opera more strongly cast. . . . All the original performers had the advantage of the instruction of the composer who transfused into their minds his inspired meaning. I never shall forget his little animated countenance, when lighted up with the glowing rays of genius; —it is as impossible to describe it as it would be to paint sunbeams.

. . . I was standing close to Mozart, who, *sotto voce,* was repeating Bravo! Bravo, Bennuci; and when when Bennuci came to the fine passage, *"Cherubino, alla vittoria, alla gloria militar,"* which he gave out with stentorian lungs, the effect was electrical, for the whole of the performers on the stage, and those in the orchestra, cried out, Bravo! Bravo! Maestro. Viva, viva, grande Mozart. Those in the orchestra I thought would never stop applauding by tapping the bows of their violins against the music stands. . . .

At the end of the opera, I thought the audience would never have done applauding and calling for Mozart; almost every piece was encored, which prolonged it nearly to the length of two operas, and induced the Emperor to issue an order on the second performance that no piece of music should be encored. Never was anything more complete than the triumph of Mozart and his *Nozze di Figaro,* to which numerous overflowing audiences bore witness.

—MICHAEL KELLY,
Reminiscences

That [*Figaro*] is a mirror of its age, as one might say of all great works of art—including Dante's *Commedia* and Milton's *Paradise Lost*—is true; but it is far more than that. It is the expression of a great individual personality with a unique experience of and attitude to life; just as I would say Proust's *À la recherche du temps perdu* is. The characters in *Figaro* are not the characters of Beaumarchais' play at all; they are entirely the creation of Mozart and the expression of his own personality in every single respect. How utterly Mozart has transformed the Countess and Susanna! And what are we to say of that miraculous creation Cherubino? Never has the dewy freshness, sensitiveness, sensuousness, and ecstasy of the human heart in the first bloom of its youth had such perfect expression!

—W. J. TURNER, *Mozart, the Man and His Works*

[In playing] the saucy character Cherubino . . . I have jumped through hundreds of windows, hidden under countless chairs, and struggled and rejoiced with his wonderful, indomitable personality. . . . I'd even go so far as to boast that the opera's overture is about Cherubino too! (When you listen to it, can't you just see him dashing about, laughing and flirting and getting into trouble?) [In *Figaro*] there's a heart in every beat, and vice versa, and never does Mozart give up on humanity. —FREDERICA VON STADE

I have just come from the Opéra Comique, where I heard *Le Nozze di Figaro.* I should go every time it is given. I know my worship of Mozart astonishes you, dear friend. I, too, am often surprised that a broken man, sound neither in mind nor spirit, like myself, should still be able to enjoy Mozart, while I do not succumb to the depth and force of Beethoven, to the glow and passion of Schumann, nor the brilliance of Meyerbeer, Berlioz and Wagner. Mozart is not oppressive or agitating. He captivates, delights and comforts me. To hear his music is to feel one has accomplished some good deed. It is difficult to say precisely wherein this good influence lies, but undoubtedly it is beneficial; the longer I live and the better I know him, the more I love his music.

—PYOTR ILICH TCHAIKOVSKY, in a letter to Nedejda von Meck

Every number in *Figaro* is for me a marvel; I simply cannot understand how anyone could create anything so perfect; such a thing has never been done, not even by Beethoven.

—JOHANNES BRAHMS

Then on to *Figaro* at the Old Vic. It's perfectly lovely, breaking from one beauty into another, and so romantic as well as witty—the perfection of music, and the vindication of opera.

—VIRGINIA WOOLF, *Diary,* 1917

144 Mozartiana

In *Figaro*, the dialogue becomes purely music and the music itself dialogue.

—RICHARD WAGNER

Figaro was given on 30 March, in Mahler's edition. It was one of his finest productions and, with *Don Giovanni*, *Fidelio* and *Tristan*, one of the sacred few he kept under his own hand and eye.

—ALMA MAHLER, in a letter, 1906

The nature of Mozart's comedy is extremely serious; that is why it plays on the heart-strings.

—PETER HALL

A *finale*, which has to be closely connected with the rest of the opera, is a sort of little comedy in itself and requires a fresh plot and a special interest of its own. This is the great occasion for showing off the genius of the composer, the ability of the singers, and the most effective "situation" of the drama. Recitative is excluded from it; everything is sung, and every style of singing must find a place in it—*adagio, allegro, andante, amabile, armonioso, strepitoso, arcistrepitoso, strepitosissimo. . . .* [This] gives not one twinge but a hundred to the unhappy brain of the poet who has to write the words.

—LORENZO DA PONTE

Why, an opera is sure of success when the plot is well worked out, the words written solely for the music and not shoved in here and there to suit some miserable rhyme (which, God knows, never enhances the value of any theatrical performance, but rather detracts from it). . . . The best thing of all is when a good composer, who understands the stage and is talented enough to make sound suggestions, meets an able poet, that true phoenix.

—MOZART

The Mozart–Da Ponte collaboration continued with *Don Giovanni* and *Così Fan Tutte.*

DON GIOVANNI
Premiere: October 29, 1787, Prague

How can one say Mozart composed *Don Giovanni*! As if it were a piece of cake or biscuit stirred together out of eggs, flour and sugar! It is a spiritual creation, in which the details as well as the whole are pervaded by *one* spirit and by the breath of *one* life.

—JOHANN WOLFGANG
VON GOETHE

After the Vienna premiere—

EMPEROR JOSEPH: The opera is heavenly, perhaps even more beautiful

Now for the Serenade 147

than *Figaro.* But not food for the teeth of my Viennese.

MOZART (under his breath): *Well, then give them time to chew on it!*

Vanity, eccentricity, fancy, have created *Don Giovanni,* not the heart.

—SCHNEIDER, music critic in the *Geschichte der Berliner Oper,* after the first performance

This opera is not for the Viennese. It suits the people of Prague better—but most of all it is written for me and my friends.   —FRANZ JOSEPH HAYDN

Mozart said, *"I did my* Don Juan *for myself and three of my friends."*
— JEAN-AUGUSTE-DOMINIQUE INGRES, written in his notebook after his painting *The Martyrdom of St. Symphorien* was badly received

Take a farmer from Essoyes to hear that masterpiece of all masterpieces, Mozart's *Don Giovanni,* he'd be bored stiff. He'd much prefer a café concert.
— PIERRE-AUGUSTE RENOIR, in *Renoir, My Father,* by Jean Renoir

Now, the *Don Giovanni,* that is different. One is confronted with an extraordinary musical creation. It is the most complete opera ever composed. It's like looking at the *Last Judgment* of Michelangelo.
— FRANCO ZEFFIRELLI

Now for the Serenade   149

The committing to paper is done quickly enough, for everything is already finished and it rarely differs on paper from what it was in my imagination.

—MOZART

Legend has it that Mozart only finished composing the overture to *Don Giovanni* the night before the first performance. Constanze kept him awake and at work by dancing with him, telling him jokes, and pouring out large and frequent glasses of punch. The copyists' ink was still wet, goes the story, when the orchestra sight-read the overture on opening night.

Among the witnesses of the first performance was old Casanova, who had come from the nearby town of Dux, and who must have had a strange experience in listening to the aria about *mille e tre,* even though his acts of seduction were based on methods different from those of *Don Giovanni.*

—ALFRED EINSTEIN, *Mozart: His Character, His Work*

Don Juan is an apparition that indeed comes to appear but never condenses into firm shape, an Individual that constantly arises but never is finished, of whose history we learn no more than what the roaring of the waves tells us.

If one conceives of Don Juan thus, everything becomes full of meaning and significance. If I think of him as a single individual . . . it seems funny that he has seduced one thousand and three maidens. If I conceive of Don Juan musically, I can then have before me the power of nature, the daemonic, which never wearies of seducing, which never stops—as little as the wind stops blowing, the sea rolling. . . . The number one thousand and three . . . gives the impression that the list is not closed, that Don Juan is still in full swing. The power of desire never grows weak.
———SØREN KIERKEGAARD, *The Stages of the Directly Erotic or the Musical-Erotic*

Mozart, Lorenzo Da Ponte, and Casanova met in Prague in 1787 during the writing of *Don Giovanni.* After Casanova's death, scholars found a manuscript in his handwriting that turned out to be the Act II sextet of *Don Giovanni*. The famous Italian adventurer was perhaps more than just an inspiration to Mozart and Da Ponte—did he actually help write *Don Giovanni?*

To many people, Don Giovanni is an anti-hero. I can't agree. Sure, he's a rake. But he dominates the opera, not just with his swashbuckling way, and the way he alters the lives of everyone who comes into contact with him, but with his grandness of spirit.

This is especially true in the final scene of the opera. Even though he knows the game is finally up, even though he's locked in the stone grip of the Commendatore, he remains defiant. "Repent!" the statue cries out. "No!" Giovanni answers. He stands his ground even as the ground gives way underneath him. . . . I think Mozart must have admired him. Perhaps he wished there was a little more of the Don in him. Maybe we all do. —SAMUEL RAMEY

Don Giovanni is the defiant counter-image of the ascetic saint.   —W. H. AUDEN

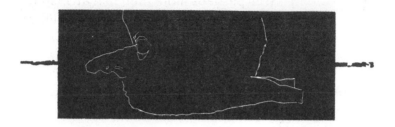

The Magic Flute remains Mozart's greatest work, for only in this did he show himself to be a German master. *Don Giovanni* is still cut to the Italian pattern, entirely so, and besides, Art, which is sacred, should never be debased in the service of so scandalous a subject!   —LUDWIG VAN BEETHOVEN

In consigning Don Giovanni to hell, Mozart was punishing his infantile and unconscious self for parricidal wishes against Leopold Mozart, and his enlightened self for parricidal wishes against the established order.   —BRIGID BROPHY, *Mozart the Dramatist*

Chopin's early fame derived from . . . the Variations for piano with orchestral accompaniment of *"Là ci darem la mano"* from *Don Giovanni*. What musician has not received profound inspiration from Mozart's realm of jest and menace, one of the half-dozen greatest of all works of art?

Gounod had himself portrayed holding the score of *Don Giovanni*. When Rossini was asked which of his own operas he preferred, he answered at once, *Don Giovanni*. Schubert and Brahms, Mendelssohn and Mahler loved the work. Chopin succumbed to it early and returned to its study all his life. He later transmitted his love to George Sand who wrote at length about *Don Giovanni* in *Le Château des Désertes*.

—GEORGE MAREK and MARIA GORDON-SMITH, *Beethoven*

After Don Juan has wounded her pride and killed her father, Donna Anna's wrath breaks out like a rushing torrent . . . in which every note in the orchestra seems to speak of her wrath and pride and actually to quiver with horror—I could cry out and weep under the overwhelming stress of the emotional impression. And her lament over her father's corpse, the duet with Don Ottavio in which she vows vengeance, her arioso in the great sextet in the churchyard—these are inimitable, colossal operatic scenes! . . . It is thanks to Mozart that I have devoted my life to music.

—PYOTR ILICH TCHAIKOVSKY,
in a letter to Nedejda von
Meck, 1878

. . . a passage in the part of Donna Anna which shocked me greatly, where Mozart had inserted a wretched vocalization which is a blot on his brilliant work. It occurs in the allegro of the soprano aria in the second act, *Non mi dir,* a song of intense melancholy . . . and yet it is made to wind up with such a ridiculous, unseemly phrase that one wonders how the same man could have written both. The words of the passage are *"Forse un giorno il Cielo ancora sentirà pietà di me* (to hope that heaven will one day take pity on me)." A truly strange form of expression for a noble, outraged woman. . . . I found it difficult to forgive Mozart for this enormity. I now feel I would shed my life's blood if I could thereby erase that shameful page and others of the same kind which disfigure some of his work. . . . Mozart has there committed one of the most flagrant crimes recorded in the history of art against passion, feeling, good taste, and good sense.

—HECTOR BERLIOZ

On February 12, 1829, during one of his conversations with Goethe, Eckermann expressed the hope that *Faust* might someday find a music appropriate to it. [Goethe's reply was]: " The repellent, loathsome, and terrifying qualities which it would have to contain are not in the style of our times. It would have to be music like *Don Juan.* Mozart would have had to compose *Faust.*"
— WOLFGANG HILDESHEIMER,
Mozart

Before describing the emotions that this incomparable masterpiece stirred in me, I ask myself if any pen can ever translate them—but at least in such a way as to give some idea of what went on inside me during those unparalleled hours, the charm of which has dominated my life like a luminous apparition, a revelatory vision.

From the start of the overture I felt myself transported into an absolutely new world by the solemn and majestic chords of the Commendatore's final scene. I was seized by a terror which froze me, with those descending and ascending scales unrolling above it, merciless and implacable as a death sentence, I was overcome by such dread that I buried my face in my mother's shoulder and whispered, "Oh, mama, what music! This is truly music!"

—CHARLES-FRANÇOIS GOUNOD,
composer of *Faust*, in
Mémoires d'un Artiste

Awestruck by Mozart, people ask how he made magic from mere scales, and they cite the slow ebbing strings at the climax of *Don Giovanni*. Then they proffer their own non-answer: He was Mozart!

A real answer: Assuming the strings *are* magic, they are not "mere" scales. Mere scales are just that, mere, and get boring in lesser Mozart sonatas. However, in his opera the composer does turn a seven note melodic minor mode into two (ascending, then descending) eight note harmonic minor passages. He immediately repeats this pattern a half-tone higher, then a whole tone higher, and so on up chromatically, ever tightening the screw with the pseudomodulatory device (or vise) much copied in today's pop songs. Meanwhile a human basso intones a pedal "A" whose color alters according to the flux of color beneath, above and beside it. These independent occurrences are melded by "abstract" chords of sustained lower bass, by a kettledrum heartbeat, and by the Commendatore's "concrete" language. Now this concrete language—Italian prose—is missing from Mozart's first and only "plant" of the menacing mood, hours earlier, in the overture. But because the plant hints to connoisseurs what is to come . . . the scales in the overture may justly be termed psychological, a word inappropriate to any wholly nonvocal music, including Beethoven's quartets.

Mozart's "mere" scale was but one of many

simultaneous happenings on his page: we may be aware of just that scale while the rest is subliminal, but the rest, while maybe magic, is analyzable magic.

—NED ROREM, *The Absolute Gift*

There are three things in the world I love most—the sea, *Hamlet,* and *Don Giovanni.*

—GUSTAVE FLAUBERT

So long as one has the Mozartian order ringing in one's ear one can also understand what is meant by saying that mathematics is frozen music, with . . . emotions, passions, breathed into mathematically calculable vibrations. Don Giovanni, Donna Elvira, Leporello, Zerlina, the Commendatore and Masetto—bright glass spheres moving about, in and out between each other, worlds resounding in infinite space. By knowing how to set them vibrating the magus Mozart could make them here attract each other, simply and sweetly, there tragically repel each other, all in their courses forming one great unison that becomes life itself, Nature itself. Who can ever adequately thank that purest of all artists for the fact that so long as his work echoes in our ears it cannot but seem to us the interpretation of some more sublime happening? —OSKAR KOKOSCHKA, *A Sea Ringed with Visions*

I would walk ten leagues through the mud, the thing I hate most in the world, to hear a good performance of *Don Giovanni.* If anybody quotes an Italian phrase out of *Don Giovanni* immediately my tender memories of the music recur to me and take possession of me. . . . Certainly no opera d'inchiòstro, no work of literature, gives me so keen a pleasure.

—STENDHAL, *Life of Henri Brulard*

Don Giovanni is the opera of operas.
—LEOŠ JANÁČEK

For the nineteenth-century romantics, *Don Giovanni* was self-evidently Mozart's greatest opera; for them it pre-echoed their own romanticism as no other opera of the 18th century did. There had been picaresque novels and plays but none that swashbuckled so outrageously, blasphemed so heartily, wrung the withers so thoroughly. When Grand Opera became popular, *Don Giovanni,* by the divine daemonic Mozart, transformed itself, with little assistance, into the proto-grand-opera.

—WILLIAM MANN, *The Operas of Mozart*

Never have I left an opera house so richly rewarded as today, when I saw so many people, notable in such different ways, in one place. The Emperor and his family were to come to the opera today, and the entire route from castle to opera house swarmed with people. "Away with these people!" With a gesture a little man in a green coat bids me attend to more attractive matters. It is Mozart, whose *Don Juan* is to be given today, to see for himself the transports into which his glorious harmonies put the audience's hearts. Who can derive more satisfaction from his own self than he? In vain would monarchs exhaust their treasures . . . these cannot buy one little spark of the feeling with which Art rewards her darling!

All men must fear death, only the artist fears him not. He will move future generations when the bones of kings have long mouldered away. And secure in these convictions Mozart could stand there, when a thousand ears were listening for every quivering of a string, every whisper of a flute. . . . Be it fanatical enthusiasm, be it genuine human feeling: enough, at that moment I would rather have been Mozart than the Emperor Leopold.

—ALEXANDER VON KLEIST,
Phantasien auf einer Reise
nach Prag, 1792

COSÌ FAN TUTTE
(Thus Do All Women;
All Women Are This Way)
Premiere: January 26, 1790,
Vienna (on the eve of
Mozart's thirty-fourth
birthday)

A miserable thing, which lowers all women, cannot possibly please female spectators, and will therefore not make its fortune.

—FRIEDRICH LUDWIG SCHROEDER,
actor, in his diary, 1790

[*Così* is] a gay and charming trifle, graceful, amusing, and inconsequential, even to the point of being preposterous. . . . In comparison with Lorenzo [Da Ponte's] previous masterpieces it has always been thought trivial.   —MARCIA DAVENPORT, *Mozart*

Artifice is the keynote of *Così*. What else could it have been? But then again, who else could have made it as unfailingly charming as the master who remains the finest artificer as well as the greatest artist whose services music ever enjoyed?

—ERIC BLOM, *The Operas of Mozart*

This libretto was denounced throughout the nineteenth century as being intolerably stupid, if not positively disgusting, and various attempts were made in Germany and elsewhere to "improve" it, or even to substitute an entirely fresh libretto on a totally different subject. In 1863, the authors of the libretto of Gounod's *Faust* adapted it to a French version of *Love's Labours Lost. . . .* [But] *Così Fan Tutte* is the best of all Da Ponte's librettos and the most exquisite work of art among Mozart's operas. It is as perfect a libretto as any composer could desire, though no composer but Mozart could ever do it justice. . . . If the realists maintain that the story is an insult to human nature, let them read the reports of the Divorce Court during the period of a war.

Such embarrassment as modern listeners sometimes do feel is due to the sheer beauty of the music itself; they cannot bear to think that it is the deliberate expression of sham feeling and . . . comically exaggerated passion.　　—EDWARD J. DENT, *Mozart's Operas: A Critical Study*

In *Così Fan Tutte,* the dying eighteenth century casts a backward glance over a period outstanding in European life for grace and charm. . . . Admittedly it lacks the grandeur of *Don Giovanni,* the brilliant and acute vigor of *Figaro* or the bright, dewy freshness of *Il Scraglio;* nor do we find there any of those solemn intimations which are heard now and then in *The Magic Flute. Così Fan Tutte* is a long summer day spent in a cloudless land by a southern sea, and its motto might be that of Hazlitt's sundial:

"I count only the hours that are serene."
　　　　　　　　　—THOMAS BEECHAM,
　　　　　　　　　A Mingled Chime

Strauss embraced *Così* with particular warmth at a time when it did not enjoy the regard it does today. His performances played an important part in promoting recognition of the work's worthiness to stand alongside Mozart's three popular masterpieces. He expressed his affection for the "superior ironies" of *Così* in an essay he wrote in 1910 on the occasion of a new production of the work in its original form.

—NORMAN DEL MAR,
Life of Strauss

During the writing of *Così Fan Tutte*, Mozart's wife, Constanze, fell ill and was sent, on doctor's advice, to Baden for a cure. Mozart thereby incurred terrible financial difficulties—and marital worries. For when Constanze started to recover, she began a flirtation which Mozart soon found out about.

I'd wish, sometimes, that you didn't make yourself so common. . . . Remember the promises that you made me, Oh God! Don't torment yourself and me with unnecessary jealousy. . . . Don't ever go alone [to the

baths]—I am terrified at the thought. . . . Have confidence in my love, you already have proofs of it—and you shall see how contented we will be.
> —MOZART, in a letter to
> Constanze

**THE CLEMENCY
OF TITUS**
(La Clemenza di Tito)
Premiere: September 6,
1791, Prague

So beautiful as to entice the angels down to earth.
> —FRANZ ALEXANDER VON KLEIST,
> 1791

Porcheria tedesca . . . (German hoggery).
> —EMPRESS MARIA LOUISA
> of Bohemia, at the
> premiere, 1791

Mozart was ill in Prague, and dosed himself ceaselessly. His colour was pale, and his countenance sad, although his merry sense of humour often bubbled into jesting, in the company of his friends.

—FRANZ NIEMETSCHEK, on the *Clemenza* premiere, *Life of Mozart,* 1798

Mozart's return to the *opera seria* had nothing of that exciting new departure which each of the five great operas shows. He was not interested in this commission, nor, one fancies, in Roman history, and Metastasio's frigid libretto made no appeal to him. His craftsmanship functions as beautifully as ever ... but it is a masterpiece in cold marble, not in the living flesh and blood he knew so well how to set in action on the stage.   —ERIC BLOM, *Mozart*

A most tedious spectacle.

—COUNT KARL ZINZENDORF

THE MAGIC FLUTE
(Die Zauberflöte)
Premiere: September 30,
1791, Vienna

The latest machine-comedy, *The Magic Flute*, with music by our kappellmeister Mozart, has been given at great expense and with lavish sets and costumes, but has failed to win the acclaim that was hoped, on account of its appalling plot and text.

—Musikalisches Wochenblatt,
September 30, 1791

The applause which *Die Zauberflöte* received in Vienna was exceptionally great. It was performed sixty-two times in succession, and the attendance showed no sign of diminishing.

—Geheime Geschichte in den
Osterreichischen Staaten,
London, 1795

Now for the Serenade 169

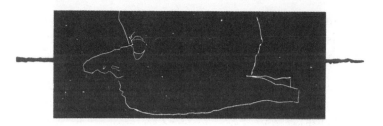

The music and decors are pretty, the rest an incredible farce. Huge audience.

> —COUNT KARL ZINZENDORF, at
> the twenty-fourth perfor-
> mance, November 6, 1791

It is fit to be performed before the greatest monarchs at the greatest festivities.

> —ANTONIO SALIERI

Die Zauberflöte was produced at Schikaneder's theatre, with that enterprising barnstormer not only announced in large type as the author, but appearing in the part of Papageno, so designed as to earn him all the evening's laughs and to put the catchiest tunes in his mouth. Mozart's name was characteristically given only in a note under the cast:

> The music is by Herr Wolfgang Amade Mozart, *Kappellmeister* and Imperial Royal Chamber Musician in Ordinary. Herr Mozart will, in deference to a gracious and honorable public, and from friendship for the author of the piece, conduct the orchestra in person today.
>
> —Eric Blom, *Mozart*

Just as Shakespeare, after the life-long anonymity of the dramatist who remains concealed behind the characters of his plays, appears himself in his last drama, *The Tempest,* so, I believe, does the human personality of Mozart appear in *The Magic Flute.*

—Bruno Walter

At the October 8, 1791, performance, Mozart sneaked backstage, while Schikaneder, as Papageno, was "playing" the Glockenspiel:

So I played a trick. At one point where Schikaneder has a pause I played an arpeggio—he was startled—looked into the wings and saw me—when it came the second time—I didn't play one—then he stopped and refused to continue—I guessed his thoughts and played another chord—then he hit the Glockenspiel and said "Shut up!"—everybody laughed at this—I believe that many people, as a result of this joke, realized for the first time that he does not play the instrument himself.

—MOZART

If we would rightly judge and perfectly enjoy the *Zauberflöte*, we must get one of the spiritualistic wizards of today to transport us to the Theater an der Wien in the year of its first production.

That *Zauberflöte* so immeasurably exceeded the demands addressed to [Mozart] that here no *individ-*

ual, but a whole *genus* of the most surprising novelty seemed born, we must take as the reason why this work stands solitary and assignable to no particular age whatsoever. Here the eternal and temporary meet for every age and people.

—RICHARD WAGNER,
Prose Works

There is no news here but that *Die Zauberflöte* has been given eighteen times, and that the house was always packed full; no person will have it said of him that he has not seen it, all the gardeners, indeed, even the inhabitants of Sachsenhausen, whose children play the apes and lions, go to see it. A spectacle like this has never been known here before; the house has to open before 4 o'clock each time, and in spite of that, some hundreds always have to go away again because they cannot get a seat.

—GOETHE'S MOTHER, FRAU
KATHARINA ELISABETH, in a
letter to her son,
November 9, 1793

Goethe himself wrote the beginnings of a sequel to *The Magic Flute;* however, it remained a fragment and was never set to music.

In my film *Hour of the Wolf,* I later tried to create the scene [from *The Magic Flute*] that had moved me most profoundly. Tamino is left alone in the palace garden. He cries, "Oh, dark night! When will you vanish? When shall I find light in the darkness?" The chorus answers *pianissimo* from within the temple, "Soon, soon or never more!" Tamino: "Soon? Soon? Or never more. Hidden creatures, give me your answer. Does Pamina still live?" The chorus answers in the distance: "Pamina, Pamina still lives."

These twelve bars involve two questions at life's outer limits—but also two answers. When Mozart wrote his opera, he was already ill, the spectre of death touching him. In a moment of impatient despair, he cries, "Oh, dark night! When will you vanish? . . ." The chorus responds ambiguously, "Soon, soon or never more." The mortally sick Mozart cries out a question into the darkness. Out of this darkness, he answers his own questions—*or does he receive an answer?*

Then the other question: "Does Pamina still live?" The music translates the text's simple question into the greatest of all questions. "Does Love live? Is Love real?" The answer comes, quivering but hopeful ... Pa-*mi*-na still lives. Love exists. Love is real in the world of human beings.

—INGMAR BERGMAN, director of a film version of *The Magic Flute*, in *The Magic Lantern*

Mozart and Schikaneder, in creating *The Magic Flute*, performed a deed of valor, for in spite of the disapproval of the higher-ups they defended their noble cause [Freemasonry]. It is, therefore, the swan-song of Masonry in Austria, an eloquent defense of those who were innocently condemned, a farewell worthy of those who were exiled, but also a magic means for Freemasonry to continue spreading in spite of all prohibition.

—ALEXANDER ZILLE,
Mozart and Freemasonry

It is therefore interesting to compare the Requiem with *Die Zauberflöte,* the Catholic with the Masonic idea of death. . . . The difference is at once apparent; the words of the Requiem insist constantly upon just that fear of death which Freemasonry had taught Mozart to overcome. . . . The Requiem, despite its beauty, can hardly be contemplated without pain. . . . It is to *Die Zauberflöte* that we must turn to know Mozart's religious feelings at their sanest and most exalted degree. —EDWARD J. DENT, *Mozart's Operas: A Critical Study*

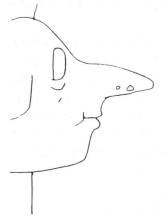

If Mozart had died before writing *The Magic Flute,* his death would have been illogical.

—PAUL KLEE, in *Klee,* by Will Grohmann

Mozart's Masonic allegory-land is a more attractive country than the *dix-huitième* Establishment countries of his other operas, at least for me, and not only musically. . . . The dramatic terrain ranges more widely, partly because of the new and diverse elevations of the religious, the mystical and the supernatural. In fact, the greatest achievement of the opera is precisely the unity of feeling that embues all of the music, from the sacred choruses and magic spells to the proto-Broadway duet—except in musical quality—concerning the future propagations of Papageno and Papagena.

The most obvious anticipations are of Weber, Wagner, the Mendelssohn of *Midsummer Night's Dream.* (The most obvious omission is Schubert, who had already been scooped in *"L'ho perduta"* from *Figaro.*) Wagner is everywhere, and all the way from *Tannhäuser* to *Tristan.* . . . The Pamina-Sarastro scene is Wagnerian, too, except that Mozart stops at the point where Wagner, already heavy breathing, would have begun to overblow.

The forerunning is more remarkable in the *Terzett* and the accompaniment to Papageno's final aria, which plagiarize and improve upon *The Sleeping Beauty;* in the choral parts and instrumental bass line of *"Bald, bald, Jüngling,"* which have been lifted from

Rigoletto; and in the introduction to *"Drei Knäbchen, jung, schön,"* which might have been borrowed from a rainy-day mood piece by Ravel.

—IGOR STRAVINSKY, *Retrospectives and Conclusions*

It was some years before this that, in order to ensure the success of Mozart's *Magic Flute,* the manager of the Opera produced that marvellous travesty of it, *Les Mystères d'Isis,* the libretto of which is a mystery as yet unveiled by no one. When he had manipulated the text of this masterpiece to his liking, our intelligent manager sent for a *German* composer to help him patch up the music. The German proved equal to the occasion. He stuck a few bars on to the end of the overture (the overture to *The Magic Flute!*), turned the soprano part of a chorus into a bass aria, adding a few bars of his own; transplanted the wind instruments from one scene to another; changed the air and altered the instrumental accompaniment in Sarastro's glorious aria; manufactured a song out of the slaves' chorus . . . and converted a duet into a trio.

When this wretched hotch-potch was ready, it was . . . printed and published in full score with the name of that profane idiot Lachnith actually bracketed with Mozart's on the title page.

In this wise, and at twenty years' interval . . . beggars in filthy rags came masquerading before the public in the rich robes of [Mozart].

—HECTOR BERLIOZ, *Memoirs*

That of which Lessing convinces us only with the expenditure of many words sounds clear and irresistible in *The Magic Flute:* the longing for light and day. Therefore there is something like the glory of daybreak in the tones of Mozart's opera; it is wafted towards us like the morning breeze which dispels the shadows and invokes the sun.

—FRIEDRICH VON SCHILLER

The sheer sound of *The Magic Flute* is of an unearthly beauty. Having completed their historic reconnaissance of the giant planets, Jupiter, Saturn, Uranus and Neptune, the Voyager 1 and 2 spacecraft have achieved escape velocity from the solar system. At a million miles a day, they are speeding into the cold, dark interstellar night. Because very little happens in the deep vacuum of interstellar space, the spacecraft are expected to survive intact for billions of years as they orbit the center of the Milky Way galaxy. Should either spacecraft one day be intercepted by an advanced interstellar spacefaring civilization, the Voyagers contain, prominently displayed, a golden phonograph record containing a wide range of information about the beings and the civilization that launched these ships. Among 118 pictures digitally encoded, greetings in many languages, scientific data, a sound essay on the evolution of life on Earth, and the brain waves of a young woman in love, there is an hour and a half of the world's great music—East and West, classical and folk. The room available on the record was too limited to be fully representative of the cultures of the Earth, and the time available to compile and produce the record was very brief. But among those who put the record together there was no dissent at all about the importance of including something by Wolfgang Amadeus Mozart. The composition selected is the only example of grand opera on the record. It is an aria sung by Edda Moser from *The Magic Flute*—fittingly, "Queen of the Night."

—CARL SAGAN and
ANN DRUYAN

180   Mozartiana

Dearest, best little Wife!
I am but just returned from the opera. It was quite as full as ever. The duetto, *"Man and Wife," etc., and the glockenspiel in Act I were encored as usual—the boy terzett in Act II in addition. But what always gives me the greatest pleasure is the* silent *approval. It is apparent that this opera is becoming more and more popular. . . .*

The time drags for me without you—as I thought it would. Adieu, *dear little wife! I hope and expect to get a line from you today, and in this sweet hope I kiss you a thousand times, and am*

> *Ever thy Loving Husband,*
> *W. A. Mozart*

Nine weeks after the first performance of *The Magic Flute,* Mozart was dead.

Requiem

LAST DAYS

Didn't I tell you that I was composing this Requiem for myself? —MOZART, December 5, 1791

Süssmayr was at Mozart's bedside. The well-known Requiem lay on the quilt, and Mozart was explaining to him how, in his opinion, he ought to finish it when he was gone. . . . His last movement was an attempt to express with his mouth the drum passages of the Requiem. That I can still hear. . . . Words fail me, dearest brother, to describe how his devoted wife in her utter misery threw herself on her knees and implored the Almighty for his aid. She simply could not tear herself away from Mozart, however much I begged her to do so. If it was possible to increase her sorrow, this was done on the day after that dreadful night, when crowds of people walked past his corpse and wept and wailed for him.

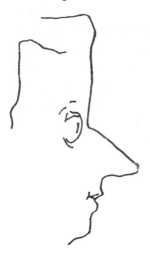

—SOPHIE HAIBL, Mozart's sister-in-law, who was present at Mozart's deathbed, in a letter, April 7, 1825

The death of Mozart before he had passed his thirty-fifth year is perhaps the greatest loss the musical world has ever suffered.

—EDVARD GRIEG

Since Death, strictly speaking, is the true end and purpose of our life, for several years I have made myself so familiar with this true, best friend of men that his image holds nothing frightening for me any-

more, but much that is calming and consoling. And I thank my God that He granted to me the blessing of providing me with the opportunity of recognizing in Death the real key to our true happiness. I never go to bed without considering that perhaps, as young as I am, I may not see the next day dawn. . . . For this supreme joy, I thank my Creator every day, and wish it to every one of my fellow-men from the bottom of my heart. —MOZART, in a letter to his father

For some time I was beside myself about his [Mozart's] death, and I could not believe that Providence would so soon claim the life of such an indispensable man. I only regret that before his death, he could not convince the English, who walk in darkness in this respect, of his greatness—a subject about which I have been preaching to them every single day.... You will be good enough, my kind friend, to send me a catalogue of those pieces to promote such works for the widow's benefit; I wrote the poor woman three weeks ago, and told her that when her favorite son reaches the necessary age, I shall give him composition lessons to the very best of my ability, and at no cost, so that I can, to some extent, fill his father's position. —FRANZ JOSEPH HAYDN, in a letter from London, 1792, to Johann Michael Puchberg, music publisher in Vienna

One day a gaunt stranger dressed in grey presented himself at Mozart's lodging with an order to compose a Requiem. It was to be called for at an appointed time and bought at a generous price, on condition that the composer should not tell a soul about the commission and the conditions under which it had been offered him. The transaction was in reality quite sim-

ple. The caller was the steward of a certain noble-
man, Count Franz von Walsegg, who dabbled in
music, wished to bestow a great work on the world
as his own, and, lacking the required invention and
skill, conceived the idea of buying it ready-made
from an acknowledged master. . . . But to Mozart, who
was probably far from well at the time and may have
been in a feverish state when the stranger called, the
incident seemed charged with the most sinister im-
port. It threw him into a state of acute depression and
foreboding. He set to work on the Requiem in a frame
of mind in which, to judge by its music, a kind of
febrile exaltation and fascination were uppermost.

      —ERIC BLOM, *Mozart*

I can assure you as a man of honor that there is no
truth in that absurd report; of course you know—

Mozart—I am said to have poisoned him; but no—malice, sheer malice; tell the world, dear Moscheles, old Salieri, who is on his deathbed, has told this to you.

—ANTONIO SALIERI, to his pupil Ignaz Moscheles, who visited Salieri in the "common hospital" where he died (over thirty years after Mozart)

Mozart's illness in Vienna in August 1784 provides an important clue to the possible cause of his mysterious death. . . . It is my view that Mozart at this time suffered a streptococcal throat infection and that this was complicated by the development of Schönlein-Henoch syndrome [an autoimmune disorder involving primarily kidneys, joints, and blood vessels]. Furthermore, Mozart at this time developed glomerulonephritis, the disease which eventually caused his death. . . .

Mozart took to his bed for the last time on 20 November 1791. His final illness had been contracted during an epidemic, probably at the [Freemason] Lodge, on 18 November and lasted 15 days. It was associated with a high fever and much sweating. During the night he complained of pain on moving in bed, and his wife noted that his feet and hands were quite swollen. . . . There were recurrent attacks of violent vomiting, especially at night, and later diarrhoea. After a week in bed he was helpless. . . . Sophie Haibl and her mother made him night shirts which could be put on him from the front, for he could not turn over in bed because of the swelling. . . .

Mozart remained conscious until two hours before his death, and said there was a taste of death on his tongue. . . . [The doctor] ordered Sophie Haibl to apply a towel, moistened with vinegar and cold water, to Mozart's forehead. There followed a violent shuddering [then] loss of consciousness. Towards midnight, he raised himself, opened his eyes wide, and then lay down with his face to the wall. . . . Mozart remained unconscious and died at about 1 o'clock on 5 December . . . and on 6 December Mozart's body was consigned to a common grave containing 15–20 corpses; no stone marked his resting place in the churchyard of St. Mark's.

—Dr. Peter J. Davies, *Journal of the Royal Society of Medicine,* September 1983

The deepest impression left by [Dr. Davies's] study is the composer's lifelong history of sickliness. From childhood on, Mozart suffered from a series of ailments that should have sucked all creative energy from him. Letters and other documents describe upper respiratory tract infections, body lesions, tonsillitis, severe toxemia, delirium, skin rash, pneumonia, typhoid fever, rheumatism, rheumatic fever, smallpox (his face was permanently disfigured by the disease), dental abcess, bronchitis, yellow jaundice, catarrh, pains in the eyes and ears, viral infection, and much else. Seldom, it would seem, was he in even moderately good health. . . .

Mere day-to-day existence must have been difficult under the burden of such painful illnesses. What could such a sick man accomplish? All Mozart did in his last four months, with body and mind disintegrating, was to compose *The Magic Flute, La Clemenza di Tito,* the Clarinet Concerto, most of the Requiem, a Masonic cantata and some miscellaneous pieces. Think of him next time you have to stay in bed with a cold. —DONAL HENAHAN

And now I must go just as it had become possible for me to live quietly. Now I must leave my Art just as I had freed myself from the slavery of fashion, had broken the bonds of speculators, and won the privilege of following my own feelings and composing freely and independently whatever my heart prompted! I must leave my family, my poor children in the moment when I would have been better able to care for them! —MOZART, on his deathbed

The Friends of Music in Prague on the 14th performed solemn obsequies for Wolfgang Gottlieb Mozart, Kappellmeister and Hofkomponist, who died here on the 5th. The ceremony had been arranged by the Prague Orchestra of the National

Theater, and all Prague's well-known musicians took part in it. On the appointed day the bells of the parish church were rung for half an hour; almost the entire city streamed thither, so that the Walsche Platz could not hold the coaches, nor the church (which can hold nearly 4,000 people) the admirers of the dead artist. . . . Solemn silence lay all about, and a thousand tears flowed in poignant memory of the artist who through his harmonies so often tuned all hearts to the liveliest feelings.

—*Weiner Zeitung,*
December 24, 1791

The world will not see such talent again for a hundred years.　　　　　—FRANZ JOSEPH HAYDN

The Mozartian legacy, in brief, is as good an excuse for mankind's existence as we shall ever encounter and is perhaps, after all, a still small hope for our ultimate survival.

—H. C. ROBBINS LANDON,
Mozart's Last Year

I should like to have heard my Zauberflöte *one more time.* —MOZART, on his deathbed,
December 1791

In the night of the fourth and fifth of this month, there died here the *Hofkammerkompositor* Wolfgang Mozart. Known from his childhood as the possessor of the finest musical talent in all Europe, through the fortunate development of his exceptional natural gifts and through persistent application, he climbed to the pinnacle of the greatest masters; his works, loved and admired by all, bear witness to this, and are the measure of the irreplaceable loss that the noble art of music has suffered by his death.

—*Weiner Zeitung,*
December 7, 1791

The artist Joseph Solman gained recognition as a painter in the mid-1930s, first with a one-man show and then as a founding member of *The Ten,* now recognized as the first coherent group of American Expressionists, which included Rothko, Bolotowsky, Gottlieb, and Ben-Zion, among others. His reputation was secured with the bold street scenes of his early years, his celebrated portraits of the fifties, and the East Villagers he painted in the sixties. In 1950 he joined the ACA Gallery in New York, where he was represented for many years. He is now represented by the Salander-O'Reilly Gallery in New York.

The recipient of numerous awards and honors, including the 1961 National Institute of Arts and Letters Award in Painting, the artist has had one-man shows in New York, Los Angeles, Chicago, Baltimore, and Washington, D.C., as well as major cities abroad, which have won him wide acclaim. His work is included in such collections as the Whitney Museum of American Art, the Phillips Memorial Gallery, the Hirshhorn Museum, the Rose Art Collection of Brandeis University, and the British Museum. His most recent shows include 1930s gouaches and 1980 collages at the Robert Brown Contemporary Art Gallery in Washington, D.C., and "Portraits from the Sixties" at the Judi Rotenberg Gallery in Boston. He currently lives in New York City.

Grateful acknowledgment is made to the following for permission to reprint previously published material:

Bantam Doubleday Dell Publishing Group, Inc.: Excerpt from *World of Ideas II* by Bill Moyers. Copyright © 1990 by Public Affairs Television, Inc. Reprinted by permission of Bantam Doubleday Dell Publishing Group, Inc.

British Medical Journal: Excerpt from "Medicine and Music" by Paton, Pahor and Graham from the *British Medical Journal,* December 20, 1986. Reprinted by permission of the British Medical Journal and the authors.

JM Dent & Sons Ltd.: Excerpts from *Mozart* by Eric Blom. Reprinted by permission of JM Dent & Sons Ltd.

Farrar, Straus & Giroux, Inc., and JM Dent & Sons Ltd.: Excerpts from *Mozart* by Wolfgang Hildesheimer. Translation Copyright © 1982 by Farrar, Straus & Giroux, Inc. Reprinted by permission of Farrar, Straus & Giroux, Inc., and JM Dent & Sons Ltd.

Alfred A. Knopf, Inc.: "Mozart, 1935" from *The Collected Poems of Wallace Stevens.* Copyright 1936 by Wallace Stevens. Copyright renewed 1964 by Holly Stevens. British Commonwealth rights excluding Canada are administered by Faber & Faber, Ltd. Reprinted by permission of Alfred A. Knopf, Inc. and Faber & Faber Ltd. Excerpts from *The Memoirs of Hector Berlioz: From 1803–1865,* translated by Rachel and Eleanor Holmes, with Annotations and Revisions of the Translation by Ernest Newman. Copyright 1932 by Alfred A. Knopf, Inc. Copyright renewed 1960 by Vera Newman. Reprinted by permission of Alfred A. Knopf, Inc.